THE COMIC SPIRIT
IN
RESTORATION DRAMA

THE COMIC SPIRIT

IN

RESTORATION DRAMA

STUDIES IN THE COMEDY OF
ETHEREGE, WYCHERLEY, CONGREVE,
VANBRUGH, AND FARQUHAR

BY HENRY TEN EYCK PERRY

NEW YORK
RUSSELL & RUSSELL · INC
1962

TO

A. D. A.

TABLE OF CONTENTS

PREFACE

ANOTHER book on Restoration Comedy perhaps demands a word of explanation, for much has recently been done both in scholarship and criticism in this particular field. Professor Nettleton in his *English Drama of the Restoration and Eighteenth Century* has given us a thoroughgoing dramatic history of the period; Mr. Allardyce Nicoll has covered the years from 1660 to 1700 with more emphasis on the minor writers; Professor Bernbaum in *The Drama of Sensibility* has traced the subsequent decline of true comedy and the rise of sentimentalism; Mr. John Palmer in *The Comedy of Manners* has drawn full-length portraits of Sir George Etherege, William Wycherley, William Congreve, Sir John Vanbrugh, and George Farquhar.* A full bibliography may be found in any book of reference (and need not be given here), but the works I have mentioned, which are broad in their scope, have been of especial use to me—particularly Mr. Palmer's treatment of the personalities whose work I wish to consider more intensively, and from a somewhat different point of view. In the following pages I have tried to analyze the comic theory and practice of the leading Restoration playwrights, with the hope that through a close study of the texts themselves I may add something to the present estimate of the

* While this book has been in the press, there has appeared a volume by Bonamy Dobrée, *Restoration Comedy 1660-1720*. Mr. Dobrée minimizes the French influence during this period and analyzes, in a very stimulating way, the psychology of the authors whose comedies I am here discussing.

position of Etherege, Wycherley, Congreve, Vanbrugh, and Farquhar in the history of dramatic comedy.

The last four authors named have formed a classic quartet ever since Leigh Hunt republished their works in 1840, and Edmund Gosse in his *Seventeenth Century Studies* definitely added Etherege to this group as the first important figure in Restoration Comedy. Gosse also made it clear that only Etherege and Wycherley can properly be called "Restoration" writers, for, although that title still clings to Congreve, Vanbrugh, and Farquhar, these three authors wrote chiefly in the reign of William III and may more correctly be termed "Orange Dramatists." A hiatus of more than fifteen years occurs between the work of Wycherley and Congreve, which materially adds to the difficulty of treating all these writers as representatives of the same historic milieu, though it still seems justifiable to take them together. Mr. Palmer has related these figures to their times. I shall attempt to examine their work in a more detached and minute way. After all, it is as dramatists that these men are chiefly known. Congreve no doubt meant it when he told Voltaire that he wished to be visited as a fine gentleman and not as an author; but Voltaire administered a well-deserved rebuke to him on this score when he replied, "que s'il avoit eu le malheur de n'être qu'un gentilhomme comme un autre, je ne le ferois jamais venu voir, et je fus très choquée de cette vanité si mal placée." Voltaire knew as well as another that the true immortality of an author had best be entrusted to his writings.

A careful analysis of the twenty-odd comedies of Etherege, Wycherley, Congreve, Vanbrugh, and Farquhar should throw a good deal of light upon their aims as well as upon their methods of work. It has been said

that no Restoration Comedy can stand having its plot too
closely scrutinized, but if that be true, so much the worse
for Restoration Comedy. Analysis does not change the
essential nature of an object, and *The Way of the World*
is still *The Way of the World*, however badly it may appear to be constructed from a technical standpoint. On
the other hand, a discussion of situations, of characters,
of dialogue, and of general atmosphere may be of use not
only in determining the excellences and the defects of
these works, and the intentions of their authors, but also
in capturing for a moment the essential spirit of English
comedy as it existed during the years from 1664 to 1707.

Now comedy is, by its very nature, a baffling and illu-
sive thing. It cannot easily be tied down to laws and
canons of criticism, because its material is as varied and
shifting as life itself. Nevertheless, in order to understand the concrete embodiments of the laughing muse, it
is necessary to have some notion of the comic point of
view. This I have attempted to give in an introductory
chapter by reviewing—necessarily briefly and incom-
pletely—the philosophy of laughter from Aristotle to the
present day, with particular attention to the two chief
theories as to the nature of human mirth. In so far as
laughter is a social force, the most concentrated and tan-
gible way of embodying comedy in an artistic form is to
set it on the stage by actors before an audience; and the
history of dramatic comedy in Greece and Rome, in
France and England is the record of the world's practical
achievement in this genre. Such a history, which can
only be baldly outlined in this book, gives the proper per-
spective for intelligent criticism of the productions of a
particular epoch, such as the latter half of the seventeenth century.

Some knowledge of contemporary social conditions is, of course, also essential to an understanding of what comic writers are attempting, especially in an age like the Restoration when they are almost exclusively preoccupied with the surface of life. In any period the comic dramatist must always draw his material from things about him, because laughter is a human thing and cannot rise above its social source, but each individual author will select a different phase of his environment for treatment and each will have a different attitude towards his subject-matter. In the body of this book I have traced the artistic career of the authors considered, seeking to show with what basic principles each started and with what conclusions he ended his play-writing, in so far as they are revealed by his practice throughout his life.

In my last chapter I have set off the highly developed Comedy of Manners against the more primitive Comedy of Situation and the less artificial Comedy of Character as they appear in English literature. In world literature the dominant figure among authors of this last kind is a Frenchman. The more one studies any period of dramatic comedy, especially the Restoration Age, where his influence was predominant, the more one is inclined to acknowledge the supremacy and genius of Jean-Baptiste Poquelin, known to the world at large as Molière. If, by indirection finding direction out, this book is able to increase and strengthen his reputation, it has amply accomplished its purpose.

THEORY AND PRACTICE OF DRAMATIC COMEDY

I.

T HE COMIC SPIRIT" has been an accepted
term in literary criticism ever since George
Meredith celebrated it in his famous *Essay on
Comedy*, originally delivered as a lecture on February 1,
1877; but a philosophical attitude towards laughter is as
old as Plato and Aristotle. Mankind seems always to
have laughed. Indeed man is known as the "laughing animal," and when we compare him with the animals or
with momentary glimpses of the divine, one can easily see
why. Man is a mixture of heaven and earth, the higher
and the lower, the spiritual and the physical. He is, in a
word, an incongruity, and incongruity is at the basis of
all laughter. Mirth of any kind is always a paradox: one
laughs in order that he may not weep, but one also laughs
because some inferior being is weeping. It is no wonder
then that the philosophers have disagreed in their diagno-
sis of such a complicated and varied phenomenon, or that
many of them from Cicero to Benedetto Croce have
frankly given up the riddle as insoluble. When moderns
like Sigmund Freud and Max Eastman are absolutely
sure that they have found the key in "gratification of re-
pressed tendencies" or "an act of aggressive resignation,"
the mind instinctively flees from the jargon of psychology
and takes refuge in the simplicity of classic philosophy.

Plato, its chief exponent, contented himself with saying in the *Philebus*, through the mouth of Socrates, that

"at a comedy the soul experiences a mixed feeling of pleasure and pain." How can it be otherwise when at one and the same time a human being exults in his superiority to the animals and regrets his inferiority to the gods? We must necessarily feel pleasure in our successes and pain in our failures; when we are affected by a combination of the two, we reach the core of the human problem—and if we do not laugh, at least we smile. The mind of man enables him to recognize these conflicting elements in his nature, but to explain why we are creatures who suffer and rejoice seems beyond the scope of mortal intelligence; to give a satisfactory explanation of that conflict would be to explain the universe itself. Fortunately the writer of comedy does not try to probe behind the veil of appearance but is satisfied with considering things as they are. Otherwise we should have no laughter in literary form, for philosophers themselves are notoriously lacking in a sense of humor. To them is left the business of evolving hypotheses to justify the *status quo*, and they have not been slow to elaborate the two parts of Plato's original dictum. They have continually sought to explain the ludicrous by emphasizing either pleasure or pain as the cause of it, but seldom by reverting to Plato's wise synthesis of the two.

Aristotle himself seeks to disentangle these opposing factors but is not wholly successful in doing so: in one place, the *Poetics*, he asserts that laughter comes from observing "some defect or ugliness, which is not painful or destructive"; in another, the *Rhetoric*, he lays it to a deceived expectation. These conflicting Aristotelian pronouncements have given rise to the two great historical theories of the comic. The first, that we are amused at the limitations of others, has been most pointedly and famously stated by Hobbes in the *Discourse on Human Nature:* "The passion of laughter is nothing else but sudden glory arising from a sudden conception of some eminency in ourselves, by comparison with the infirmity of others, or with our own formerly." The second, that we laugh nervously from disappointment, finds classic expression in Kant's *Critique of Judgment:* "Laughter is an affection arising from the sudden transformation of a strained expectation into nothing." It is variations on these two theories that make up the history of comic philosophy, but their resolution is not yet. Perhaps they never can be definitely resolved, and perhaps it is not necessary that they should be. When all is said and done, "at a comedy the soul experiences a mixed feeling of pleasure and pain."

The similarities rather than the divergences of the pleasure and pain theories may help out our understanding of the comic. In each case the suddenness of the changed condition is largely responsible for the burst of laughter; in each case there is an implied or expressed comparison between the amusing incident and something that is inferior or superior to it. In other words, the phenomenon of laughter demands that two dissimilar facts be brought into close relationship with one another so abruptly that the reasons for their difference cannot be analyzed. The mind is not given sufficient time to rationalize an apparent incongruity, although it takes some glimmerings of brain power to appreciate the incongruity at all. Hence mirth is not entirely an intellectual matter, but there is always present in it an intellectual factor, without which it could not exist. The more subtle and ingenious is the point of a joke, the more important is the function of the human understanding, but even in the most primitive forms of horseplay there is a latent appeal to the intelligence.

Take for instance the common incident of a man who slips on a banana skin in the street and falls into the gutter amid the guffaws of passersby. Their amusement may be interpreted either in terms of the erect superiority of the laughers, or because falling in such a way and at such a time is, to their minds, neither suitable nor natural. Yet whatever the motive, one would hardly laugh if the fall of the man were gradual instead of instantaneous; nor if he had just said, "Now I am going to slip on a banana peel"; nor if our own fall, or that of a friend, were in question. Unusual philosophic detachment and at least a temporary subjugation of the emotions are necessary to an appreciation of the joke when it is upon one's self, but even a conscious effort cannot always achieve this comic point of view.

"A sense of humor" is too deep-rooted to be governed wholly by thought, but nevertheless it is a phenomenon of consciousness which depends primarily upon mental processes and which belongs only to reasoning creatures. The sudden juxtaposition of incongruous details enables the intellect to draw a swift and inevitable conclusion that here is food for laughter, whereas an emotional emphasis upon any one specific fact means upsetting a well-balanced, rational view of life. There must, of course, be frequent divergences from such a norm, but as long as the norm is kept in mind for purposes of comparison, the divergences from it only serve as material for honest and wholesome mirth. When our emotions interfere with this impersonal detachment, we begin to lose the comic point of view, or as Horace Walpole has epigrammatically and pregnantly expressed it, "The world is a comedy to those that think, a tragedy to those who feel."

This pointed observation clearly reveals the limitations of comedy. Thinking is certainly not all of the world or even the most important part of it, yet it is the essence of the Comic Spirit. "If you believe that our civilization is founded in common sense," wrote Meredith, "(and it is the first condition of sanity to believe it), you will, when contemplating men, discern a Spirit overhead. . . . It has the sage's brows, and the sunny malice of a faun lurks at the corners of the half-closed lips drawn in an idle wariness of half-tension. . . . Men's future upon earth does not attract it; their honesty and shapeliness in the present does; and whenever they wax out of proportion . . . ; whenever it sees them self-deceived or hoodwinked . . . ; whenever they are at variance with their professions . . . ; whenever they offend sound reason, fair justice; . . . the Spirit overhead will look humanely malign, and cast an oblique light on them, followed by volleys of silvery laughter. That is the Comic Spirit." That rather is Meredith's rhapsody on the Comic Spirit, a rhapsody which, when carefully analyzed, falls into line with Walpole's more trenchant dictum. The Comic Spirit is an ally of "common sense," "sound reason," "fair justice": that is, it is primarily the possession of "those who think." The trouble is that no man thinks all the time in this world and that, as a result, the Comic Spirit has really a very restricted range of operation.

Certainly the even, unimpassioned temper necessary for the dominance of the comic point of view can sometimes be attained, but it is generally of sporadic occurrence and brief duration. One can see often enough offenses against reason and justice; it is far more difficult to regard them with equanimity and fair-mindedness. The most insidious factor in destroying the comic equipoise is disgust that human beings should so far diverge from the happy mean. How can men be so dominated by avarice, lust, hate, or pride that they completely forget the other elements in human life? This is the basic prepossession of the reformer, it infuses him with *saeva indignatio*, and he becomes an out-and-out satirist, like Juvenal, Swift, and Voltaire. Or else the comic artist is all too human, sympathizes with the failings of mankind, and becomes emotionally involved on their side rather than against them; in which case his work comes to take the form of humor and is recognizable under the varying guises of Pantagruelism, Quixotism, and Shandyism. The Comic Spirit proper shuns the two extremes of Satire and Sentiment. It attempts to maintain an impersonal detachment, based upon intellectual grounds. It does not wish either to scorn or to sympathize, for scorn and sympathy imply judgment, and who are we to judge? Its essential preoccupation is to know. "Wit" is the centre of its being, and "wit" is by derivation connected with the idea of knowledge. "In a world where much is to be done and little is to be known," the Comic Spirit must necessarily have a rather precarious existence.

II.

Comedy fares best in the open. Laughter is essentially a social thing and flourishes where private feelings must be temporarily effaced for the public good. Personal joy and grief cannot always be indulged in the arena of life, where an infinite number of impersonal encounters make up so large a part of human activity. And it is these very impersonal relationships that in the multiplicity and variety of their details furnish the richest material for the Comic Spirit; it observes them constantly, combines them incongruously, and allows the onlookers to draw their own conclusions. Hence the stage is the proper habitat of the Comic Spirit. Here, before a varied audience, men and women may be represented in the innumerable ridiculous situations of human life, the spectators may laugh at their own foibles revealed in other people, and purging, not by pity and terror, but by "a mixed feeling of pleasure and pain" may endlessly result.

The history of "comedy" bears out an emphasis upon its dramatic phases. Its very name is derived from κῶμος or a village revel, a primitive social gathering intended to make its participants forget their individual concerns in the midst of public absurdities. The vague, unformed songs and dances of which these revels were composed gradually shaped themselves into stereotyped incidents, frequently repeated, and lo! dramatic comedy was born. The process was slow, of course. It took centuries for the informalities of natural social intercourse to become sufficiently stabilized for expression in an artistic form. The first real comedy is as much shrouded in obscurity as the first real ballad, and indeed this analogy is far from imperfect. Bit by bit, one man with an especially marked comic sense came to predominate over his fellows in the invention of humorous material, stamped his personality on the celebrations of his own community, and in this way became a real creative artist. In many places and at many times this procedure must have taken place, until there existed a vast number of authors whose works were never committed to posterity and whose names are consequently quite unknown to us. Because of the fact that a play is essentially a transitory production, dependent

on actors and an audience, authorship of drama has always been a dubious claim to fame. If the exact limits of
Shakespeare's writing have never been definitely determined and if even today our commercial successes in the
theatre owe much to their producers and actors, how shall
we wonder that the prehistoric Molières were, if not
mute, at least inglorious and that their works have been
quite lost in the dark backward and abysm of Time?

Their form has best been preserved to us in the plays
of Aristophanes, which as we have them are certainly
primitive and elementary enough, but which mark the
first literary development of comic drama. Further refine-
ments came in the "new comedy" of Menander, were
taken up by Plautus and Terence, and through these authors became definite factors in the literature of the Re-
naissance. All comedy since that time in Italy, in Spain,
in France, and in England has been built on the classic
tradition, though more sophisticated changes in matter
and manner have, of course, been inevitable. With in-
creased knowledge and technique, the dramatists grew
discontented with type figures and attempted further and
further to humanize their material. The comic sense became constantly finer and the potentialities of the finished product correspondingly greater, until the culmination of this genre was reached in seventeenth-century
France with the work of Molière.

In England the process continued beyond its climax.
Ben Jonson and the other Elizabethans had not had the
benefit of Molière's influence and example, but their successors in the Restoration period came after the great
Frenchman and profited by that fact. If anything, they
profited too much, for in developing the thoughtfulness
of laughter they often neglected its basic humanity. They

ceased to be interested in the comic as it pertained to human life in general and tended to occupy themselves with the comic as it appeared upon the surface of a highly polished and fundamentally insecure civilization. Their milieu was ideally suited to their accomplishment, but neither the spirit of their age nor its representation in literature can pretend to an equal association with the best which has been thought and said in the world.

Here again the social quality of laughter is a determining factor, for any writer of dramatic comedy must be much affected by the intellectual calibre of the group of people to whom he is appealing. A primitive throng must be appealed to by primitive methods, but as the mentality of an audience becomes developed, the more subtle will be the incongruities that the dramatist is called upon to expose. Plautus and Terence had a more difficult task, and at the same time a greater opportunity, than did Aristophanes; Molière's audience was perhaps ideal in its combination of intelligence and humanity. The court of Charles II and his immediate successors was too sophisticated and unscrupulous to evoke the deepest and truest comment on life from the purveyors of its amusement. One does not look for philosophers in an assemblage of pleasure-seekers; the most that can be found there is an occasional soul that instinctively revolts at the very superficialities in which he is indulging. For perfect detachment we must seek spiritual withdrawal from the world, and of that not many a Restoration gentleman was capable. If he had the perceptions of an artist, he might, like Etherege or Congreve, smile tolerantly at his surroundings, or like Wycherley he could attack them unmercifully at the same time that he was very much a part of them. A real change in point of view was necessary for complete disapproval of existing conditions, and such a point of view meant an outlook on life so serious that comedy withered under its gaze.

Works like those of Vanbrugh and Farquhar are evidences that this change ultimately took place, but the causes of it must be sought elsewhere. After an age of license and misrule a reaction was bound to occur, a reaction which, as far as the theatre was concerned, concentrated itself in the person of Jeremy Collier. In 1698 he published his *Short View of the Immorality and Profaneness of the English Stage*, and from that time on the "immorality" of Restoration Comedy has been generally considered its most salient characteristic. The dramatic fare offered by Restoration Dramatists to their audiences stunk so violently in the nostrils of Collier and of his spiritual successor, Lord Macaulay, that the finest examples of English comedy are only just now recovering from the effects of their disapproval and once more receiving unprejudiced attention. Not that many people yet read for pleasure the plays of Etherege or Wycherley, of Congreve, Vanbrugh, or Farquhar, much less that they are generally seen upon our commercial stages, but that they are again beginning to be acted here and there, that they are now commonly studied in our universities, that connoisseurs are beginning to talk of them above their breaths, and that the world at large is ready to accord them more than a *succès de curiosité*. It is high time. In an age which prides itself on having done away with moral barriers, an honest examination of the work of the Restoration Dramatists need not bring a blush to the cheek of modesty. It should be considered not as moral or unmoral—a problem which never disturbed its authors—but from the point of view of the Comic Spirit, from which they themselves chiefly regarded it.

Yet even so, the moral implications of a study of Restoration Comedy are not so far removed from the aesthetic ones as might at first be supposed. If, as Ruskin constantly asserts, there is a real relation between art and morals, one cannot expect to find the greatest literature springing from a civilization not itself of the highest type. The critical error involved in condemning the work of Restoration Dramatists as immoral consists in attacking their subject-matter, which they were bound to draw from contemporary manners. The scene of Mr. Horner's china is suitable material for literature if it be true to life, but its final value depends upon whether it is properly used for comic purposes. This question of the informing spirit behind a work of art is delicate and elusive, for it, too, is inseparably connected with the historic background. It can perhaps best be isolated from considerations of time and locality and weighed in the balance for its intrinsic worth by comparing it with other points of view towards similar material, which in this case means by comparing it with other manifestations of dramatic comedy. For that purpose it is necessary to have some notion of the nature of laughter in theory and practice. Then by seeing wherein the Restoration authors diverge from the happy equilibrium of pleasure and pain, where they fall into vehement satire or maudlin sentiment, their real importance can best be gauged. It may be that their best attempts to establish the even balance of comedy have not the solidity and power for which the genius of a Molière is demanded, but their limitations may be as significant as their abilities. Nor can they with impunity be criticized too harshly, for this much may definitely be stated in regard to them: whatever else they may or may not do, the playwrights of the Restoration furnish us with the best examples in English drama of that finely tempered and infinitely precious thing which we call the Comic Spirit.

SIR GEORGE ETHEREGE
1635?—1691?

SIR GEORGE ETHEREGE is the author of only three plays, but they are all three important in the history of comedy and all three infused with the Comic Spirit. *The Comical Revenge; or, Love in a Tub* appeared in 1664; *She Would if She Could* in 1668; *The Man of Mode; or, Sir Fopling Flutter*, after a lapse of eight years, in 1676. The intervals between these dates show how very casual was Etherege's contribution to the theatre, and perhaps they also explain the vast improvement of each play over its predecessor. The titles in each case reveal the author's special preoccupation with his material and hence suggest the development of Etherege's technique as a comic dramatist.

I.

The Comical Revenge is the trick played by a pert maid, Betty, on a rascally French valet, Dufoy. Dufoy is sick of the pox, and in order to explain his ailing condition, he lays the blame for it upon Betty's scorn of his advances. Now, as a matter of fact, he has never even spoken to Betty, who thereupon determines to revenge the lie upon his own head. She catches him dead-drunk and has him locked into a tub, curiously contrived without a bottom and with a hole in its top, through which Dufoy's neck is made to pass. Thus imprisoned, he becomes the butt of the sprightly Betty and her friends until another episode in the plot procures his release. This, it can be easily seen, is mere farce, a situation fairly amusing in itself, but one which from its very simplicity cannot be long continued without wearying an audience. Indeed only four scenes are devoted to this incident, as compared with ten long ones occupied with the affairs of the four romantic lovers in the play. The pseudo-serious plot which concerns them need not be discussed here, as it is not essentially comic in its nature nor well adapted to display the genius of Etherege. The historically interesting experiment of writing in rhymed couplets he never afterwards repeated, perhaps having learned by experience that his talents did not lie in that direction. He seems to have been ill at ease when trying to write in the grand style and to have realized that both he and his audience would be better pleased if he gave free rein to his humorous fancy. Pepys bears witness that the success of the play was caused by its farcical qualities and exactly defines its limitations when he writes on January 4, 1665: "Mr. Moore and I to 'Love in a Tubb,' which is very merry, but only so by gesture not wit at all, which methinks is beneath the House." As we shall see, there were elements in the play that Pepys evidently did not appreciate, but he was right as to its essential nature, which is boisterous and thin.

In his next attempt to write for the stage Etherege seems deliberately to have tried to remedy this defect in his fable, for *She Would if She Could* is based on a stock situation capable of far greater development than are the "Tub" scenes in his first play. Lady Cockwood is desirous of playing her husband false and has selected the personable Courtal as an instrument in her design. Courtal, unfortunately for her Ladyship, has got himself into deeper water than he intended, and as a result he has to spend most of his time avoiding the attentions she heaps upon him. So it is that the heroine would but cannot. Her attempts to entrap the unwilling gallant, and his evasions, are necessarily somewhat monotonous dramatic material, but Etherege displays considerable ingenuity in varying these intrinsically similar situations. The first time that Lady Cockwood and Courtal are alone together, he arranges to have the lady's husband return unexpectedly; the second time their tête-à-tête in the New Exchange is interrupted by two attractive young ladies. Each interruption is the occasion for a renewed rendezvous, but after three acts of these complications Etherege realized that he must introduce new matter. Thereupon Lady Cockwood begins to see Courtal's real attitude and to act the part of Potiphar's wife, at the same time trying to take up with another young man. She succeeds in causing a fight between her husband and Courtal but fails in obtaining a lover, so that at the end of the play she chooses a domestic reconciliation rather than further unsatisfactory intrigues.

It can be seen that, though uneven, these complications are diverting and ingenious; moreover, they give a body to the play in which they occur that is quite in harmony with its author's general outlook on life. Etherege's notion of infidelity in matrimony as a comic subject was entirely in accord with the ideas of his time, though in this particular case the laugh is only incidentally on Lady Cockwood's simpleton of a husband. She herself is the central figure of the piece, an object for mirth because she does not deceive her husband as she hopes and plans to do. It is only incidental that, while engaged in her amorous pursuits, she appears to the world as a model of virtue. This circumstance has caused Mr. Gosse to refer to

her in his *Seventeenth Century Studies* as a "female Tartuffe," but in so doing he has mistaken a minor point for
a major one. The true humor of Lady Cockwood depends
upon the fact that she is obviously a pursuing woman
whose undue eagerness prevents her from successfully
landing her prey. There is a grain of human sympathy in
her portrayal, which makes one think of, and long for, the
touch of Molière; but, on the whole, no one need be disturbed by the moral implications of the plot. Lady Cockwood's heroic efforts and most unheroic failure to achieve
her purposes make her a satiric figure, set up to ridicule
the ambitions of many an unhappily married woman. As
such, she is a finished portrait and prepares us not to be
surprised at the turn which Etherege's creative ability
took in his next play.

The title character in *The Man of Mode; or, Sir Fopling Flutter* is a further working-out of the method employed with Lady Cockwood. She is a fashionable lady
balked in the pursuit of pleasure; Sir Fopling is a beau
who makes himself ridiculous by overdoing his pretensions to style. He is perfectly hit off in the descriptions of
him before he appears upon the stage: "He is indeed the
pattern of modern foppery. . . . He was yesterday at the
play, with a pair of gloves up to his elbows and a periwig
more exactly curled than a lady's head newly dressed for
a ball. . . . What a pretty lisp he has. . . . That he af-
fects in imitation of the people of quality of France.
. . . He is a person indeed of great acquired follies."
According to Sir Fopling a man ought to dress well,
dance well, fence well, be amorous, discreet, but not too
constant—a creed which he perfectly follows when we
see him upon the stage. He is just come back from France,
like many a Restoration courtier, and he brings with him

not only French clothes and French words, but French manners and French affectations. Undoubtedly, too, he had, like his creator, acquired a French taste in drama. As good an example as another of Sir Fopling's absurdities is his treatment of his English footman, honest John Trott. "Trott, Trott, Trott! there's nothing so barbarous as the names of our English servants," and as the unfortunate Trott happens to come from Hampshire, he is rechristened with the name of that county, the sound of which better befits the mouth of a man of quality.

In drawing this figure Etherege has reached into one of the higher realms of the ridiculous: he has definitely entered the province of satire. If, like other great art, comedy is both to please and instruct, its instruction must come from making absurd the ugly and imperfect. At its most serious it attacks such basic defects in human nature as avarice, hypocrisy, misanthropy,—to take only a few examples from the master of French comedy; at its more superficial, as in Etherege, it hits lightly on habits and customs that jar on the sensibilities of a well-balanced intellect. The method of the satirist is to select some characteristic human failing, to elaborate it, to create a personage in whom this exaggeration is portrayed, and to set such a typical figure in action. This process explains at once why satiric characters rarely seem to be human beings unless they are differentiated from the mass by their author's sympathy and affection. Lytton Strachey's *Eminent Victorians*, for instance, are no more than straw figures, in whom he can attack human weaknesses; but, in spite of himself, this ruthless critic has partially succumbed to the charm and personality of Victoria, the "Faery Queen." Without such a human leavening of the satirist's scorn, his characters will soon harden into types, unrecognizable as flesh and blood people, mere puppets to which suitable Jonsonian epithets may be applied as surnames: Sir Frederick *Frollick*, Sir Joslin *Jolley*, and Sir Fopling *Flutter* are examples that need no further explanation than their titles to characterize them.

With his figures once decided upon, the satiric dramatist needs only to put them in action, preferably leading them into situations where they will fare badly, in order that the intended moral may be pointedly brought home and that the audience may be entertained in the process. Sir Fopling, for instance, is shown pluming himself on his new clothes, giving an exhibition of his dancing powers, and paying court to a lady on the Mall. In the last-mentioned matter he is especially unsuccessful, as the object of his attentions is only playing with him and the next day drops him quite summarily. This is the worst thing which happens to the Man of Mode, a fact that gives an important clue to the chief weakness of the play in which he figures. He is really not an integral part of its plot (he does not even appear until the third act), but a distinct figure introduced for purely satirical purposes. Nevertheless, he is so keenly drawn as to run away with the play's title and with one's interest in the work as a whole. Etherege did an excellent piece of work in creating this typical fop with a freshness and originality not even to be matched in Vanbrugh's more finished picture of Lord Foppington.

II.

As a contrast to this picture—and what complete satirist ever failed to embody in another character the virtues which his protagonist lacks?—Etherege gives us the real gentleman of fashion in Dorimant. Dorimant has been thought to be a picture of the author himself or of the notorious Earl of Rochester, but, at any rate, he is the direct antithesis of Sir Fopling and a proper foil for him. Again Etherege is drawing his type picture from the life about him, the men of his own time whom he personally knew, but this time, instead of satirizing, he is holding up a model for his audience to copy. Dorimant is a rake, of course, but he is a rake in the grand manner, a rake of whom Etherege distinctly approves. He is the finest example of the ideal courtier to be found in any of the author's plays, although a similar figure had already been sketched in the Sir Frederick Frollick of *The Comical Revenge* and the Courtal of *She Would if She Could*. It is worth noting how alike are the "heroes" of these three plays and how alike too are the situations in which they find themselves. In fact, it seems as though start as he would with farce, comedy intrigue, or satire, Etherege could never finish his plays without putting the emphasis upon contemporary social life. There lies his real interest —and our interest too—and there his sense of comedy is strongest. An examination of the difficulties in the way of each of his fine gentlemen, and their method of resolving them, will throw some light upon the customs of the time in their lighter aspect: that is, as they furnish suitable material for the Comic Muse.

Sir Frederick at the beginning of *The Comical Revenge* has been out on a wild drinking party the night before and is suffering from a combination of bad headache and unpaid debts. The hackney coachmen, the linkboys, the fiddlers, and the chambermaid employed in the course of the recent orgy arrive to be satisfied for their part in the proceedings, which ended with the assault of a whore's lodgings and "a general massacre on the glass-windows." The maid is come ostensibly to berate Sir Frederick but really to make a renewed appointment with him on her mistress's behalf. Meanwhile he intends to pass the time with his present wench but is diverted from her by a friend who tells him of new game. A wealthy widow has become enamored of his person and has arranged to dine that day where he can meet her. Sir Frederick is considerably elated at the news and departs from his rooms with infinite zest for the adventure, already quite forgetful of his last night's escapade.

She Would if She Could opens more mildly but in the same vein. Courtal and Freeman are complaining that life is unconscionably dull because they must always consort with the same ladies and can find no new faces in the town. An interlude is provided by Lady Cockwood's maid with a message for Courtal from her mistress, who is just come up to London. The merry but stupid husband, Sir Oliver Cockwood, drops in; the maid is hurried into the wood-hole; and when the danger of detection is past, she escapes safely, leaving Courtal to ponder on how to conduct an intrigue which has already become wearisome to him. This action expounds the initial situation and sets the main plot in motion, but it does more, because Sir Oliver casually informs the young men that two new young ladies are in town. They are kinswomen of his friend Sir Joslin Jolley and are lodging at the same house as the Cockwoods. Courtal and Freeman prick up their ears and snuff the scent. Courtal's relations with Lady Cockwood will make a meeting easy, if not inevitable. The two gentlemen—and the audience—look forward to new complications.

Dorimant's troubles in *The Man of Mode* have also to do with debts and women. The shoemaker and the orange-woman clamor to be paid, but they are waved aside with the grand air that so well becomes a Dorimant. He cannot be bothered with trivial matters just now; in time all will be adjusted. One of his former mistresses, the illiterate Molly, writes him to ask for a guinea "to see the operies," but his chief trouble is with Mrs. Loveit, his present flame. When the curtain rises we see him trying to write her a love-letter—with poor success because his heart is not in it. His mind is now occupied with Belinda, a conquest which he is just on the verge of making and does actually make before the play is done. And then, as if it were not enough for the hero to have these three affairs on his hands, the orange-woman tells him that a beautiful young heiress is sighing for him. It is a little difficult to keep Dorimant's intrigues straight in one's mind. Molly, Mrs. Loveit, and Belinda are the mistresses of past, present, and future respectively; Harriet Woodvil is the young heiress who is ultimately to become his wife. Such a resolution for the plot is in accordance with the conventional comedy ending, which demands that the most hardened philanderer should settle down at last with some pure young girl and live happily ever after— so far as the audience can be expected to know. However, in this case Dorimant is attractive enough to win the heart of any woman, and Harriet Woodvil, as we shall see, is quite a match for him. In fact, just as Dorimant is Etherege's final portrait of the Restoration gentleman, so is Harriet his ideal of what the Restoration young lady ought to be. In each case the picture had been already roughly sketched in his earlier work.

III.

In *The Comical Revenge* Sir Frederick Frollick is a
vaguely drawn Dorimant and the spirited young Widow
a first impression for Harriet Woodvil. She is in love
with Sir Frederick and arranges a meeting, but the opportunity once made, she meets his advances with banter and
ridicule. This is the only way in which any fine gentleman can be won. He always thinks of himself as irresisti-
ble, and his interest is only to be piqued by apparent indifference and opposition. There is no better situation in
the whole realm of comedy than the one thus developed.
Without any real overthrow of natural laws, the ordinary
relation of pursuing male and resisting female is here
subtly reversed. The girl continually gets the better of
the man, until ultimately she forces him to capitulate, as
she has herself done in her heart long ago. Sir Frederick
has been told that the Widow loves him, and he never
appears to doubt it; the game is to get her to admit her
love for him openly, in his presence. He serenades her,
thus gains admittance to her house, and diverts her with
a masque, but as soon as the entertainment is over, she
hopes that he'll leave her to her rest. Expostulation does
no good, and in the end he departs with the biting *mot:*
"Go, go to bed, and be idle, widow; that's worse than any
misfortune I can meet with." Yet words are but poor
things; Sir Frederick does leave, and the Widow is victor
in the first round. So is she in the second. Sir Frederick
feigns death to get her sympathy, but just as she begins
to bewail him Dufoy comes running in with his tub, Sir
Frederick jumps up, and the laugh is on the Widow's
side again. Finally Sir Frederick scores by a pretense of
being arrested for debt. Dufoy again causes a revelation

of the true state of affairs, but not until the Widow has already given herself away by paying her gallant's supposed debts.

The resolution of such an intrigue is one of the most difficult problems with which the comic dramatist has to deal. The gentleman having been brought around, how shall the lady be made to reverse her position and to yield gracefully without too great a loss of dignity? A huggermugger fifth act conclusion is always possible, but Etherege honestly seems to be seeking, albeit somewhat clumsily, for a logical outcome. In the last scene of his first play the Widow is still angry at having been duped, and Sir Frederick still conscious that he is not a complete victor. He plays his trump card, departure. The Widow calls him back: "Stay, Sir; let us shake hands at parting." He returns readily enough, and the situation is definitely saved by the interposition of a third party, the Widow's brother: "Sister, I long have known your inclinations; give me leave to serve you. Sir Frederick, here, take her; and may you make each other happy." Thus the honor of both parties is saved, and despite mutual expostulations they join hands for the final curtain. The fine gentleman has so nearly met his match that a real high comedy situation has been evolved: an evenly gauged battle of wits has almost resulted in a stalemate. It is a distinct contrast to such "thoughtful laughter" to see, in this same play, the absurd Dufoy capering around the stage in his tub and to behold a stupid Puritan knight easily gulled by two conventional swindlers. These farcical plots depend on the simplicity of one character, at whose expense the jest comes; a higher kind of amusement is caused by laughter so elevated into the realm of thought that one never quite knows whether the joke is on one's self or the other fellow. This is the category into which Sir Frederick and his Widow fall, and theirs is the one situation that occurs in all three of Etherege's plays.

It is even doubled in *She Would if She Could*. Here there are two young men, Courtal and Freeman, and two young ladies, Gatty and Ariana, an arrangement which makes exposition easier for the dramatist. He can show us the two young men discussing their boredom in town, and the two young ladies, just up from the country, resolving to set out on amorous adventures. It is easy enough to make one of the girls more adventurous than her friend and so to outline their plan of campaign: they are to put on vizards, go to the Mulberry Garden, flirt with any men that they can find there, and trust to their ingenuity to get off scot-free. The scene in which they do so is inimitable and has often been quoted as the best in the entire play. It is full of wit and verve; it is cleverly planned and brilliantly executed. The twist in it comes from the fact that the young men excuse themselves from the encounter with the unknown vizards on the plea of business, but really to go and meet Gatty and Ariana in their own persons. The girls will not let them off, however, without a solemn oath that they will speak to no other women until they all four meet again the next day. The resulting scene in the ladies' lodgings may readily be imagined, but actually it does not live up to the promise of its ingeniously contrived initial situation. The men recover from their astonishment sufficiently to offer a weak excuse that introduces astrology and conjuring, but their explanations are neither convincing nor amusing.

In fact from this point the double plot peters out, perhaps just because it is double. It takes some time to discover whether Courtal is to fall in love with Gatty and

Freeman with Ariana, or *vice versa*, and when one does realize the lay of the land, it seems after all a matter of small importance. There are so many fireworks of wit, and so little pretense of real feeling, in the story that one scarcely cares about its outcome. The jealous Lady Cockwood may send the men letters purporting to be from their respective girls, the men may hide in a closet in Lady Cockwood's house and be discovered there by the young ladies, it really does not concern us either sympathetically or critically. One point which should be noticed, however, is the way in which the final capitulation on each side is managed. Whereas in *The Comical Revenge* the interest centres in how the Widow gives in, here it is equally in the surrender of the men. They never propose formally but at last suggest an armistice for the discussion of terms. While negotiations are in progress, Sir Joslin, the kinsman of Gatty and Ariana, brings home two new beaux for them: one a disreputable rake, and the other a woman of the town in man's clothes! The company is, of course, suitably shocked at the disclosure of these identities, and to protect the girls from another such insult Courtal and Freeman avow their honorable intentions to Sir Joslin; they would probably not have done so on less provocation. The young ladies are naturally not too eager to admit that they are in love, but it is obvious that they must capitulate, and without delay. At first there is talk of a month's probation, but as the curtain falls, immediate marriage is in the air and the older men are full of jests about it. Again the gentlemen are the ostensible victors, but in reality it is the ladies who win, as they usually do at the end of a comedy of intrigue. We can only regret that in this play the author concerned himself with intrigue to such an extent that, after an act or two, his characters become mere puppets and no longer bear much resemblance to live men and women. There is no pretense of emotional values in the love scenes, and the resulting action, if more than funny, is considerably less than human.

This error is avoided in *The Man of Mode*, which in this, as in every other, respect is Etherege's masterpiece. Its plot has intrigue and plenty to spare, but that does not interfere with the perfect simplicity of the wit combats that take place between the lovers, Dorimant and Harriet Woodvil. Sir Fopling himself is almost entirely removed from the serious plot of the play, which serves merely as a framework on which to hang barbed satire and brilliant repartee, the chief ingredients of this particular high comedy. Repartee, however, brilliant as it may be, is never satisfying unless it is more than mere intellectual exercise. If it does not at least suggest an underlying emotion, its flash consumes the dry tinder of which it is composed. The danger of wit lies always in its tendency to subdue the human feelings, a danger into which Restoration Comedy in general and Etherege in particular often fall. Yet in *The Man of Mode* our author seems, for the moment, to raise his love scenes to an emotional level utterly unattained in his earlier work. It may not be a completely convincing passion, but in their first interview Harriet says to herself after Dorimant's remark about her change of expression: "I feel as great a change within; but he shall never know it"; and at their second meeting the hard-hearted Dorimant confesses *sotto voce:* "I love her, and dare not let her know it." It is this concealed love for one another issuing forth in the defensive armor of conversational warfare which makes the chief charm of the Dorimant-Harriet scenes, where in a felicitous combination of verbal fencing and suppressed emotion Etherege does his most skillful dramatic writing. It is hard to know where to quote from these delightful interviews in order best to give their spirit, but the description each gives of the other brings their first talk to a brilliant conclusion:

Dorimant. As I followed you I observed how you were pleased when the fops cried, *She's handsome, very handsome, By God she is*, and whispered aloud your name, the thousand several forms you put your face into; then, to make yourself more agreeable, how wantonly you played with your head, flung back your locks, and looked smilingly over your shoulder at 'em.

Harriet. I do not go begging the men's, as you do the ladies' good liking, with a sly softness in your looks and a gentle slowness in your bows as you pass by 'em—as thus, sir;—(Acts him.) Is not this like you?

The beau mocking the coquette, and the coquette mocking the beau—was there ever a more admirably conceived self-indictment of the social group? When Dorimant does get bolder and speaks of love, then Harriet is at her most satirical. She says that if he *will* talk on that idle subject, she will put on a serious look, turn her head carelessly away, drop her lip, let her eyelids fall, and so forth and so forth. For Harriet is a clever and sophisticated actress. She torments and mimics Dorimant, as we have seen, and she plays another entertaining part in the serious plot that concerns Young Bellair.

Old Bellair and Lady Woodvil have arranged a match between their children, utterly regardless of the fact that both Young Bellair and Harriet have disposed of their affections elsewhere. This parallel situation makes the two young people conspirators at once: they enter into a formal compact never to marry one another and set about fooling their respective parents to the best of their ability. They first have recourse to the trick later made famous by Tony Lumpkin and Constance Neville, pretending to be quite ready and willing to marry one another. So when they are observed, Bellair puts his head on one side, plants his right foot firmly on the ground, and adjusts his belt, as his supposed timidity ripens into impassioned love-making. Harriet, for her part, acts the demure maiden by leaning against the wall and looking bashfully down upon her fan; then she brightens up a bit, fans herself, and looks kindly on her swain; finally she smiles, flings her body forward, and falls back in a loud spasm of laughter, covering her face with her fan. It is a charming little comedy, this of the fan, which the lovers must act to perfection, for they hoodwink their observers up to the point where Bellair and his true young lady are prepared to elope and thus obtain parental permission after the event.

This side-intrigue also figures in the Dorimant-Harriet story, as it serves Dorimant with an excuse for his formal proposal of marriage; and Dorimant is the most difficult of all Etherege's heroes to be brought to the lure. Bellair is already married, but Harriet does not know of the fact and Dorimant pretends not to. It is then apparently half out of chivalry—to save her from Bellair—that he offers her his hand and heart, but what is begun with an ulterior motive may easily be continued in deadly earnest. Dorimant is soon hopelessly involved, and one waits for Harriet to follow his lead. She is in no hurry, however, and proves to be as difficult for her lover to capture as was the Widow for Sir Frederick Frollick. Indeed Dorimant gets no more from her to the end of the play than vague encouragement. She must go back to the country with her mother, and if her ardent suitor can for a short time forswear the delights of the town she will receive him in Hampshire at "a great rambling house that looks as it were not inhabited, the family's so small; there you'll find my mother, an old lame aunt, and myself, sir, perched upon chairs at a distance in a large parlour, sitting moping like three or four melancholy birds in a spacious volery." And she will promise nothing, for after a promise anything you do is already expected from you and doesn't get half the welcome that an unlooked-for favor does. While as for hope—Dorimant may hope if he wants to, for that depends on himself, not on her, and so what good would it do her to forbid it? The final curtain leaves our hero in this unsettled state of mind, but the audience has the satisfaction of hearing Harriet tell her mother that she never could have married another man, and of hearing her mother give a reluctant consent to the match.

This latter feat is another feather in Harriet's cap, because Lady Woodvil has conceived a great dislike for Dorimant. She has heard that he is the prince of all the devils in the town and won't have his name mentioned in her presence, much less consent to see him. So the clever Harriet, realizing that in high society (as well as in artificial comedy) a great deal depends upon a name, has her lover present himself to her mother as Courtage, the fashionable flatterer of old ladies. This ruse works to perfection, as does Hastings's later toadying of Mrs. Hardcastle, and for a time gains Dorimant admission to Harriet's society. When all is finally discovered, Lady Woodvil is in a tearing rage, but Harriet calms her by tact and a show of filial respect. She says that, much as she may love Dorimant, she would never marry him without her mother's consent, a statement, which, whether true or not, completely softens Lady Woodvil's heart. Nor is it difficult to believe that Harriet meant just what she said, and that she also knew it was politically a move in the right direction, for Miss Woodvil is by no means a designing and selfish heroine. Nowhere in the play, except where she very humanly exults over Dorimant's discarded mistress, does her wit get the better of her good nature. Affectation is with her no good substitute for affection. When we are first introduced to her, she is refusing to prink over her toilet as her maid wishes her to do and violently criticizing those who powder and paint and patch. That women should set up for beauty in spite of nature! That is the keynote to Harriet's view of life, but fortunately she does not have to test the theory in her own case. The gods have already given her all the gifts that womankind desires, and it is enough to say that they have not spoiled her in the process. "Wild, witty, lovesome, beautiful, and young," as Dorimant describes her, she is the most attractively drawn heroine in any of Etherege's plays.

IV.

It is significant how in each of his comedies the figure of a charming woman dominates the piece. Dufoy may cause the easiest mirth by his odd plight in *The Comical Revenge*, Lady Cockwood may be the centre of intrigue in *She Would if She Could*, Sir Fopling Flutter may be *par excellence* Etherege's crowning achievement in satire; Sir Frederick Frollick in the earliest play is certainly a noble cavalier, Courtal and Freeman in *She Would* are remarkable for their constancy in love, Dorimant was the finest gentleman that had yet appeared on the Restoration stage; but in all of these plays the heroine runs away with the audience's heart. It must be noticed first that, whatever their ostensible subject, at bottom these comedies all depend upon a similar situation, the pursuit of a young, beautiful, and wealthy woman by a fine type of courtly gentleman; and secondly it is remarkable that in every case the woman comes off with the laurels. Her triumph is not obvious to be sure, because each time the man is successful in winning her, but at bottom the fact is self-evident. For it is always the woman who first falls in love, who tantalizes her victim until he becomes interested in her, who finally gets a declaration from him, and who melts not too easily into his arms at the last. This is Etherege's comic formula, set forth with its bare bones in the case of Sir Frederick Frollick and his Widow, somewhat involved and weakened when Gatty and Ariana capture Courtal and Freeman, but reaching a glorious climax in the encounters of Dorimant and Harriet Woodvil. Shakespeare had formulated it for Benedick and Beatrice; Dryden had already employed it in *Secret Love; or, the Maiden Queen;* Congreve was to perfect it with Mirabell and Millamant; Shaw has done it, for our own day, in *Man and Superman;* it is Etherege's distinction to have used it so persistently that we identify it with his notion of comedy.

He might begin with a practical joke, a thwarted intrigue, or a satire on contemporary manners; he always ended with a duel of sex. It is not sex treated in the heavy-handed emotional manner of the "problem play," but sex in its lighter and more impersonal aspect. He takes a man and a woman in love with one another, with no bars and impediments to their marriage except those set up by their own self-consciousness and pride—a much more common human situation than that developed by a serious triangular plot. These two lovers must have minds of a fine enough calibre to realize that people can, as in the higher levels of society they often do, wrap their true feelings in a cloak of words. The characters themselves need not appreciate the humor of such emotional evasions, but the author of their being must do so. The gods may laugh at humanity's silly equivocations, but it takes a man of genius to reveal to the rest of us the absurdities of our petty lives. The uncultivated person can never see the humor of his own existence until it is compared with some higher standard. We may all laugh at Dufoy in his tub, because tubs are not our natural garments; it takes a keener critical faculty for us to laugh at ourselves in the persons of Dorimant and Harriet, because we may not know that we are all awkward and embarrassed when it comes to meeting our match in the opposite sex.

Etherege, from his own experience we must suppose, realized this fact and its corollary, that the keenest fun comes from the closest fight. Strife, when human emotions are not too closely involved, is always a comic spectacle, because it is contrary to that ideal condition of life which the intellect predicates as desirable. The more evenly matched are the opponents, the more ridiculous is the situation. Nor can intense sympathy be created in a struggle where the antagonists are basically fond of one another, for in that case their hostility is too incongruous. Two men or two women rarely find themselves in this paradoxical situation, as it can be prevented by the interposition of a little common sense; but between a man and a woman reason is of no avail. There is a sex-hatred or a sex-fear which, as Strindberg shows us, often exists side by side with the most intense love and into which the most intense love often transforms itself. This phenomenon the comic dramatist seizes upon as the most ludicrous fact in all this ludicrous existence of ours, and he sets an isolated example of it upon the stage to amuse the finely tempered spirits in his audience. He is not necessarily satiric or bitter in doing so; in fact, the more feeling he can instill into his characters, the better for him in the long run. Only he must be sure that he never loses that mental detachment essential to the comic dramatist, which permits him to see all mankind as animated puppets in the hand of a master showman. A man and a woman, violently in love with one another, but refusing to admit it, however unhappy they may be themselves, are always a ridiculous spectacle to the intelligent observer. This fact Sir George Etherege apprehended sympathetically, he was able to demonstrate it on the stage, and as a result his three plays are important manifestations of the Comic Spirit.

WILLIAM WYCHERLEY
1640?—1716

THE dates of the four plays written by William
Wycherley are extremely difficult to determine.
The chief cause for this confusion is Wycherley's own statement as made to Pope and repeated by
Spence in his *Anecdotes*. "The chronology of Wycherley's plays I am well acquainted with," Spence makes
Pope say, "for he has told it me over and over. *Love in
a Wood* he wrote when he was but nineteen; *The Gentleman Dancing-Master* at twenty-one; *The Plain Dealer* at
twenty-five; and *The Country Wife* at one or two-and-thirty." As Wycherley was probably born in 1640, this
would make the dates of his plays 1659, 1661, 1665, and
1671-1672 respectively. To this chronology, however,
grave exception must be taken. Macaulay took great pains
to show that the composition of *Love in a Wood* in its
present form cannot have preceded 1666; *Le Misanthrope*,
on which *The Plain Dealer* is based, did not appear until
the same year; and there is a critique of *The Country
Wife* incorporated in *The Plain Dealer*, a fact which
makes it appear that the latter play was written after the
former.* Of course, there is always the possibility of interpolation and revision, but the weight of the evidence
seems to favor ruling out Spence's second-hand testimony
as unreliable. Wycherley probably wrote his plays not

* Mr. Dobrée takes the well-known position that *The Plain
Dealer* preceded *The Country Wife*, but he does not advance any
new evidence on this point.

much before their first performances on the stage, about which there is also much disagreement, but which seem to have taken place as follows: *Love in a Wood* early in 1671, *The Gentleman Dancing-Master* later in the same year or early in 1672, *The Country Wife* in 1672-1675, and *The Plain Dealer* somewhere between 1673 and 1676.

I.

Of these four plays the last two are so immensely superior as practically to contain in themselves Wycherley's entire contribution to English dramatic literature. The first two are frankly prentice work. They show glimmerings of the genius which was later to manifest itself so powerfully in *The Country Wife* and *The Plain Dealer*, but their plan is trivial and superficial by comparison. *Love in a Wood; or, St. James's Park* hinges upon a case of mistaken identity. Sir Charles Sedley's successful comedy of *The Mulberry Garden* may have suggested to Wycherley the possibilities in renewing this old theme because of the vogue for ladies to wear masks in public places: at any rate, he dressed two girls in mourning; gave each of them a lover, one jealous and one inconstant; set the masked girls and the inconstant lover in the vicinity of St. James's Park; and the trick was turned. In *The Gentleman Dancing-Master* his story is even lighter and less original. The central situation of this play comes from Calderon's Spanish comedy of *El Maestro de Danzar* and concerns a clandestine love meeting, which, on being discovered by the young lady's father, is turned by her wit into a dancing lesson. The suitor's difficulties in posing as a dancing-master furnish the chief material for laughter, but whereas in Calderon's play the whole intrigue is lifted into the higher aether of love and honor, to Wycherley the humor of the situation depends merely upon Gerrard's foolish appearance in his disguise. In the Spanish original there is some regard for the happiness and the feelings of the unfortunate hero, but Gerrard's uncertainties about his lady's affections are only used to heighten his ludicrous predicament.

This difference makes clear at once in what direction Wycherley's ability lay. He was at his best when painting dryly and dispassionately a man or woman caught in an embarrassing situation, either by chance (as in the case just cited) or, more subtly, by reason of their own mistakes. In the latter contingency a study of character and motives is immediately involved. A person who gets himself into trouble because of his own actions must have some fault, or at least some defect, which renders him out of place in a smoothly organized society. From this arises the question of a norm and deflections from it; we are in fact in the sphere where comedy merges into satire. Take, for example, the first indications of this attitude in Wycherley's early work. The most put-upon character in *Love in a Wood* is Sir Simon Addleplot, "a coxcomb, always in pursuit of women of great fortunes." He is an utter simpleton, and hence his disposition gives rise to the most obvious kind of satirical humor. He disguises himself as a clerk and works for Alderman Gripe, hoping thereby to win for himself the hand of Martha, Gripe's daughter. Now Martha has another suitor, one Dapperwit, who pretends friendship to Sir Simon in order to gull him. The disguised Sir Simon brings love-letters from Martha to Dapperwit, supposing all the time that Dapperwit is wooing for Sir Simon in his own character. We have then the extremely amusing spectacle of a man who is near his own ladylove every day, carrying love-letters to another man in order to get the latter's aid. It is almost inconceivable that there should ever really exist such an "Addleplot," the nadir of stupidity, but Wycherley creates him and makes him the butt of every one else in the play. Of course, in the end he is discomfited, after helping Martha to escape from her father's house. Then, much to his chagrin, she gives her hand to Dapperwit—as she had said all along that she was going to do!

Nor is Dapperwit such a fortunate man as he seems. He too is an object of ridicule. He thinks himself better than other men by virtue of his wit, with which he rails upon them when they are absent and insults them when they are present. He does a whole set of variations on the very word "wit," to explain what it means and to show how it should be employed. These variations are all very clever in their way, but they are spoiled by Dapperwit's knowledge that they are so. Wit must of its very essence be casual and of the moment; make it the *raison d'être* of existence and you destroy its iridescent bubble, which should serve only as the ornament of life. Therefore wit cannot take precedence of love, though Dapperwit tries to make it do so. "I am thinking what a wit without vanity is like. He is like—he is like—," and he keeps Martha waiting for the marriage while he decides that a wit without vanity is like a picture without shadows, a face without patches, or a diamond without a foil. This vanity of his makes him an easy mark for laughter. He is so proud of his wench, so anxious to display her to his friends, and so eager to appear at his best before her that when she turns him off, his chagrin is excessively apparent. Our laughter comes from the fact that he is not a neutral character nor a sympathetic one—who laughs at

Hamlet when he loses his mistress?—but frankly an absurdity now made more absurd. Ill luck is piled upon him later as well, for though he marries Martha, he no sooner does so than he discovers that all she wanted was a father for her unborn child. For no other possible reason would she have thrown herself away upon a wit! Dapperwit consoles himself with the thought that he will have her dowry, but there he was reckoning without his father-in-law, Gripe.

Alderman Gripe is probably the most finished satirical figure in the play. He is by no means the character most important to the story, but this is not strange, for *Love in a Wood* was Wycherley's first effort and it is extremely difficult for a beginner to weld satire and plot together. Alderman Gripe is a Puritan—always a target for the Restoration Dramatists—smug, self-righteous, and hypocritical. His god is money, and his byword "privacy" in sin. "I love privacy in opposition to the wicked, who hate it," he says, and it is this desire for a good reputation, regardless of the facts, which brings about his undoing. It is not necessary to go into the revolting details of the scene in Mrs. Crossbite's house; suffice it to say that Gripe's fleshly weaknesses deliver him over into the hands of two bawds, who have him completely at their mercy. As the whole affair is to cost him £500, he is torn between his avarice and his desire for respectability, but money can be regained and a good name never; so the bawds have it all their own way. This gruesome scene must be read to be appreciated. In it we see foreshadowings of the savage indignation that was so indelibly to mark Wycherley's maturer work, a horror of diseased souls and a fiendish delight in persecuting them. Gripe's position is made worse when, after he has paid the black-

mail money, his sister sees him in the park with Lucy
Crossbite, and so his reputation as well as his fortune is
seriously damaged. He can think of but one way to mend
them both at one stroke, to marry Lucy. This ignoble solution has two other advantages: it may result in his having an heir and so in excluding Martha and Dapperwit
from a share in his fortune (one thinks here of Wycherley's own second marriage in 1715 and his nephew's
mortgaged estates); "besides, 'tis agreed on all hands,
'tis cheaper keeping a wife than a wench." Such is the
cynical conclusion of Gripe's share in the plot. He seems
sure to live as unhappily ever after as he deserves. What
more can a victim of whores and bawds expect?

The women connected with Mrs. Warren's profession
are really the successful protagonists of *Love in a Wood*,
and this very fact shows how low an opinion Wycherley
had of their victims. Martha and Lucy, Mrs. Crossbite
and Mrs. Joyner rise superior to Addleplot, the simpleton, Dapperwit, the fop, and Gripe, the hypocrite. They
also take in one of their own sex, my Lady Flippant. She
is a widow in reduced circumstances, who must remarry
a fortune or else give up her establishment, her fine
clothes, her lodgings, and her coach. It is the thought of
losing her coach which especially breaks her heart and
determines her on renewed matrimonial efforts. Her plan
of campaign, to rail on marriage that she may not seem
too keen to try it again, is a further incongruity and as
such adds greatly to the amusement of the spectators.
The Lady Flippant has various victims in the course of
the play, but it is Sir Simon Addleplot upon whom she
counts as a last resort. She is much disturbed on learning
that she has been flirting with him from behind her mask
in St. James's Park and even more put out to discover

that he is the clerk who has made too free with her person. Sir Simon, of course, has no money either, so that when Martha turns him down, he is only too anxious to take up with Lady Flippant. Each is under the delusion that the other is extremely rich, a delusion well nourished by Mrs. Joyner, who in the end brings about the match. In truth, to see Mrs. Joyner in the first scene of the play cajoling first Lady Flippant, then Alderman Gripe, and finally Sir Simon Addleplot in quick succession gives at once the key to the sardonic humor of *Love in a Wood*. When knaves fall out, the less knavish come into their own. There is honor among thieves, but not among the characters of a true comedy, who must by their very nature be trying to get the better of one another. It is a world, not so very unlike the real one after all, where the fittest survives and the most put upon is the most radically defective. "Like the lawyers," says Mrs. Joyner, "while my clients endeavor to cheat one another, I in justice cheat 'em both." There may be discussion about what is justice and who should get it, but Wycherley knew for certain that it is always a cause for merriment, innocent or otherwise, to see one man's wits give way before the surer and truer ones of his intellectual superior.

II.

The same formula holds for the discomfiture of the satirized characters in *The Gentleman Dancing-Master:* Don Diego and Monsieur de Paris, father and betrothed respectively of the heroine, Hippolita. Paris is the greater dupe, for he is led, not indeed to woo for Gerrard, the hero, as in the case of Dapperwit-Sir Simon Addleplot, but actually to bring about the first meeting of the lovers. Hippolita wants a man (she doesn't care much who) and hearing Paris praise Gerrard, she tells him to take a message from her to that handsome young gentleman. Paris thinks it a practical joke on Gerrard and willingly accedes to the request, not realizing that in so doing he is introducing to his fiancée a formidable rival. The way in which Hippolita hoodwinks her father into thinking Gerrard a dancing-master sent to her by Paris has already been discussed; this is the basis of the intrigue and lasts for the better part of the three central acts of the play. At the end Paris again takes a part when Gerrard's masquerading has been discovered. Feeling responsible for the affair, he thrusts Gerrard, Hippolita, and a parson out of the room, while he explains to Don Diego how it happened; but by the time that his explanation is over, the lovers have been married and all is in readiness for the final curtain. The hapless Paris consoles himself by a liaison with Flirt, a woman of the town, who is quite as exigent as a wife and somewhat more expensive to maintain. His final situation may be a trifle more honorable than that of Alderman Gripe, who deliberately marries a whore, but it is much less advantageous financially. Such is the difference in the fates that Wycherley allots to the hard-hearted Puritan and the soft-headed fool.

The weakness in the character of Paris satirically considered is that his worst misfortunes do not come directly from his chief weakness, an affectation of French manners. He has just come back from France, a Sir Fopling Flutter in embryo, but he is less of a fop and more of an imitation Frenchman than Etherege's famous character was to be. He thinks that a man is of no account unless he has a French tailor and a French valet-de-chambre, goes to a French eating-house, sings French songs, swears French oaths, interlards his conversation with polite

French words, can dance, can play at ombre, and carries a snuffbox about with him. Paris's Gallicisms are pronounced to the point of absurdity, and they are emphasized at every turn by the Spanish ways of his uncle, Don Diego. Don Diego is really a prosperous English merchant, who has adopted Spanish customs, as Paris has done French ones. It is Don Diego's seclusion of his daughter in the stately Spanish way that causes her to desire a lover and so starts the plot of the play moving; otherwise his "humor" does not affect its action in the least. It is the old story of plot and satire existing side by side, but having very little connection with one another. In this play Wycherley has his Calderon plot and his satire on nationalities, of which the latter seems to predominate in his mind. There is a digression against the Dutch, à propos of almost nothing at all, and a constant comparison of the Spanish and the French. Don Diego and Paris are continually used to set each other off, most strikingly in the scene where Paris is made to abandon his French dress and assume a Spanish outfit. His piteous appeal to be allowed to retain his pantaloons and his cravat are of no avail; he is even compelled to take lessons from a blackamoor as to the proper Spanish way of walking and bowing. This scene is of comparative unimportance dramatically, but one suspects that to Wycherley's mind it was the most amusing and significant in his entire play.

III.

It is the elaboration of a scene like this or that of Alderman Gripe's discomfiture which made it possible for Wycherley to turn from his early comedies to such infinitely superior work as *The Country Wife* and *The Plain Dealer*. In these later plays, satire—and satire was

undoubtedly Wycherley's forte—assumes its true importance as the backbone of the plot. *The Country Wife*, for
example, is built around the idea that jealousy is petty,
mean, absurd, and ultimately fatal to its own ends.
Wycherley's treatment of the theme is a combined version of Molière's *L'École des Maris* and *L'École des
Femmes;* it is to English comedy what *Othello* is to English tragedy. Here once for all we can see what may happen in any well-regulated English society to the man who
is jealous beyond the bounds of common decency. Pinchwife, as his name implies, is such a man. He has married
a simple, demure country girl upon the supposition that
sophisticated town women make false wives but that ignorance and modesty are incorruptible. "He's a fool that
marries," Pinchwife asserts, "but he's a greater that does
not marry a fool." Unfortunately business brings him up
to town; one night he takes his wife, Margery, to the
play; and though they sit in the pit, irreparable harm is
done. In the first place, Margery likes the looks of the
actors; and in the second, one of the spectators, the notorious Horner, likes the looks of Margery. Now Horner
is accustomed to get what he wants in this world, and the
way in which he gets Margery is the subject of the
comedy.

He would never have been successful without the jealous simplicity of Pinchwife to aid him. When Margery
wants to go to another play, her husband explains his re-
fusal by telling her a gallant fell in love with her when
she was there before. Then when she insists on going out
to walk, Pinchwife dresses her up as a boy, thus making
it impossible for him to keep her away from Horner's per-
sistent attentions. Horner does carry Margery off with him
from the New Exchange, and though no harm is done,

Pinchwife goes through all the agonies of cuckoldom, much to the amusement of the audience. He is too jealous to be a sympathetic figure, almost too jealous to be a real one, so that one may laugh at him as at Jealousy personified or as at a typical example of all jealous husbands. In this way no one's feelings are injured, the spectators are purged by honest mirth, and a mirror is held up to all Pinchwives in the audience. Certainly it would be an incredibly stupid husband who would initiate his wife into the possibilities of letter-writing as does Pinchwife. "Don't I know that letters are never writ but from the country to London, and from London to the country?" says Margery in her artless way, but her husband insists that she write an insulting letter to Horner. That she has wit enough to substitute a love-letter and make her husband carry it, is not, on the whole, very surprising; that, when discovered, she lays the blame on Alithea, Pinchwife's sister, is to be explained by the assistance and advice of a pert maid. This maid also plans the trick by which Margery is taken to Horner's lodgings, disguised as Alithea, and as a result of which Horner is successful in carrying through the intrigue. Margery's innocence reveals the truth to Pinchwife, who again endures all the suffering of a deceived husband, only this time—and hence less comically—with a basis of fact to go on.

The Comic Spirit is recaptured when Pinchwife again believes something different from what has actually occurred; only in the new situation he is really a cuckold and does not know it. A quack doctor, employed for the purpose, assures the company that Horner is a eunuch and that no jealous husbands need have any cause to fear him. Pinchwife is dubious for some time, but Margery's testimony seems to satisfy him. At first the truthful

young girl cannot tell a lie and nearly ruins the stories
set forth by the deceitful city folk, but ultimately she
learns that the truth may sometimes do more harm than
good and confirms all that the quack has said. So we leave
Pinchwife at the end of the play, a deceived husband, unconscious of his own position. He has not learned all of
his lesson, but he has come to realize that keeping one's
wife in bondage will not necessarily make her dutiful and
obedient. The reformation of Pinchwife would be the
subject for a serious, and probably a sentimental, drama,
but Wycherley wisely leaves that part of the story to his
audience's imagination. As a matter of fact, it is improba-
ble that Pinchwife could ever be made to change his
ways, a typical character cannot do that; the most that
the satirist can hope for is that other men may laugh at
the jealous husband and try to be less like him themselves. If a whole audience consciously struggles against
the vice that they have seen ridiculed upon the stage, the
comic dramatist becomes of necessity an uplifting force
in his community. At any rate, we all may laugh at
Pinchwife, whether we recognize ourselves in him or not,
and laughter is always good for the soul.

Yet lest any one fail to get the point of his play, Wycherley has stated it all over again in the sub-plot. "As
dull as a single plot in a play," is a phrase from Etherege,
and it is quite clear that English theatre-goers have never
demanded "unity of action" on the stage. In fact, they do
not like it. Every Restoration Comedy has two or three
threads of plot, and when, as in *The Country Wife*, there
is a conscious attempt to pull them together, the result is
often not very felicitous. Sparkish, the central figure in
the sub-plot, is the exact opposite of Pinchwife, a man so
extreme that he refuses to be jealous even under the most

obvious provocation; he deliberately throws his friend and his fiancée together and then cannot believe that they have come to like one another. Sparkish is a would-be wit, a fop, and a fool, the logical outcome of whose history would be for him to lose his mistress through lack of sensible and necessary precautions. Molière with his basic philosophy of "nothing too much" would have made Sparkish's trusting nature as fatal as Pinchwife's jealous one, the opposing manifestations of the same great human principle. Wycherley, however, is afraid that if he shows Sparkish as too unselfish he will invalidate his principal point, the evils of jealousy, so he makes Alithea, Sparkish's young lady, an abnormally moral soul. As long as her lover believes in her, she cannot be false to him, even though she has come to love another; not until Sparkish succumbs to the green-eyed monster will she agree to give him up. It is all brought about by a trick. Pinchwife shows Sparkish the letter written to Horner by Margery, but purporting to be from Alithea; on this purely circumstantial evidence Sparkish reverses his whole position, flies into a temper, and says such cutting things to Alithea that she feels justified in breaking with him. Thus the sub-plot appears to be another example of the horrors of jealousy, but it is really just the opposite: if Sparkish's stupidity had not already cost him Alithea's love, she would not have been so eager for an excuse to get rid of him. Wycherley is false to his characters here in an effort to set forth a moral truth, and in the process he inevitably loses his hold on his audience. The Sparkish-Alithea plot in *The Country Wife* is much too inconsistent to be instructive and much too saccharine to be amusing. Sparkish's follies in the early part of the play are well-ordered comedy, but when Alithea begins to be the dominant figure, smiles give way to tears and our interest dissipates itself in yawns. Fortunately she is a character of secondary importance, for Pinchwife, Margery, and Horner refuse to be ousted from the centre of the picture.

One shudders to think what would have happened had the scrupulous Alithea actually gone to the lodgings of the unscrupulous Horner, as Pinchwife supposed that she had done. An amazing scene must have ensued, for Alithea is as soft and sentimental as Horner is dry and witty. He is, in fact, the ideal hero for a Restoration Comedy: he has no illusions and apparently no emotions; certainly he has no vices aside from purely animal ones. It is he who gets the better of the fools and dolts each time, in fact he is used as a touchstone to reveal their weaknesses. Without Horner, Pinchwife could not have been outwitted; without Horner, Margery would never have learned the ways of the world; without Horner, we should not have had the humorous characteristics of the Fidgets and the Squeamishes so well brought out. They are the folk whose failings are exposed by the report of Horner's impotence which is going around the town and which Pinchwife alone seems not to have heard. Sir Jasper Fidget believes it implicitly and therefore is quite willing to allow Horner access to his wife. Lady Fidget and Mrs. Dainty Fidget also believe it and have no use for such an odious wretch. Mrs. Squeamish believes it, and Old Lady Squeamish even allows her granddaughter to go to Horner's lodgings, where the famous scene of "Mr. Horner's china" takes place. By this time Lady Fidget has been informed of Horner's true condition, and the change in her conduct is amazing, as is that of the other ladies when they come to learn the facts.

As Horner has prophesied, his plot discovers the amorous women by their aversion to his reputation and then endears him to them when they learn the truth, because their good names have been so well safeguarded. To each of the three, Lady Fidget, Mrs. Dainty, and Mrs. Squeamish, he declares that it is for her alone that he has caused the false report to be given out, but later they all compare notes and an angry scene ensues. By that time, however, Horner does not care, for he has already achieved his ends. "You are all three my false rogues," he says, and Sir Jasper and Old Lady Squeamish are his dupes too, not to mention Margery and Pinchwife. If to fool all the people all the time be the first requisite for a hero of satirical comedy, Horner most successfully attains that ideal. He is never beaten in the course of his intrigues, he never suffers, and correspondingly he never really loves. He is the means by which the prudes are exposed and the jealous husbands punished. He is Wycherley's method of enforcing his satire. Since in this play all the complications depend upon sex relationships, it follows logically that Horner must be without a peer in these matters. He is not the author's complete ideal, and it is most unfair to Wycherley to say so; Horner himself is of small account in Wycherley's view of life, for he was created merely to embody a normal antithesis to Pinchwife's mania for possession. He is simply the winner in the comic game played in *The Country Wife*, in which the stakes are the loyalty of wives, the cards the characters of husbands. If, like Pinchwife, they regard their wives as their freehold, they are bound to lose, as Pinchwife does. The victor may appear to be a Horner, but it is really the life principle asserting itself in concrete terms. In this play the terms happen to be merely sexual; such is the critical explanation of Mr. Horner's china.

IV.

The Horner of *The Plain Dealer* is Manly; like Gulliver among the Lilliputians, he is the gauge by which the characters in Wycherley's last play are measured. He is not, like Horner, a purely sexual creature, the natural born foe to conjugal jealousy; he is an enemy to all sham and pretense, to all repressions of nature, which means practically to all organized society. "Of an honest, surly, nice humor," Wycherley describes him, and his character is set forth in action at the very opening of the play. We first see him thrusting the smooth-tongued Lord Plausible out of his lodgings and then almost immediately engaged with Freeman, his lieutenant, in a theoretical discussion of man's position in society. Freeman expounds the normal view of compromising with one's environment; Manly is all for plain dealing, *i.e.*, speaking the truth and shaming the devil. This dialogue bears a marked resemblance to that between Alceste and Philinte in the initial scene of *Le Misanthrope*, from which play Wycherley took the plot, if not the spirit, of his comedy. The difference in the attitude of the two dramatists has been frequently recognized but not always sufficiently explained, for it is not only a difference in manner but in point of attack. In Molière the satire is directed against the unsociable Alceste, but in *The Plain Dealer* Manly is the honest figure and the rest of the world is wrong. Wycherley sympathizes with his chief character and speaks through his mouth, as the author's contemporaries at once recognized. They nicknamed him "Manly" Wycherley and the "Plain Dealer," probably much to his gratification, for in the person of his hero Wycherley has embodied all that he supposed best in his own character.

Very different was the case with Molière! If "l'homme aux rubans verts" was intended as self-portraiture, it is a picture of the author's foibles and weaknesses. Molière had too good sense to suppose that the individual could ever be successful in setting himself up against the rest of the world. He realized that man was primarily a social animal and that he must adapt himself to living among other such animals. Any one who offends against this law is ludicrous and must be laughed out of court: the hypocrite, the miser, the affected fool, the hypochondriac, but above all the misanthrope, for he who hates his kind is the chief enemy of humanity. It requires infinite breadth of view and balance of mind to come to this belief, and almost as great strength of character to stick to it among the shifting currents of this world. Yet when once this detachment of attitude has been achieved, the finest manifestations of the Comic Spirit are within your grasp. To see one's self as ridiculous—and we are all ridiculous in our bilious, misanthropic moments—demands genius of the kind that was Molière's, a genius inimicable to a narrow and one-sided view of life. If the object of satire be yourself, then it is only doing a piece of necessary justice to show up the strength as well as the weakness of your position. This Molière has done so supremely well in the first scene of *Le Misanthrope* that at the end of it one is not quite sure which is right, Alceste or society. It remains for the rest of the play to answer "society" in tones as firm as they are honest, as uncompromising as they are fair. Molière constantly sees Alceste both as a reasonable being and as the ridiculous plaything of the gods. He holds the balance true between sympathy for the misanthrope's private character and the unrelenting justice of public common sense.

Wycherley does quite otherwise. He has not Molière's equanimity of temper and depth of wisdom. He is not an urbane satirist but a vicious one. He looks about the world, sees evil everywhere, and at once comes to the conclusion that the man who forswears human society is the man of sense and poise. He ceases to laugh kindly at the follies of mankind; instead he denounces them violently and in no uncertain terms. To such lengths has he gone in *The Plain Dealer* that the result, if a more trenchant satire, is a less finely balanced comedy than *The Country Wife*. To pick out one human failing, like jealousy, and to make a mock of it, is both fair and amusing, but to strike out blindly at all the deceits of the world and the flesh is to suggest that you consider yourself superior to the rest of mankind. *The Plain Dealer* is a larger canvas than *The Country Wife*, but from the very nature of its plan it cannot have the perfection and finish of Wycherley's earlier comedy, which from every literary point of view must be considered his masterpiece. It is this relation between the plays which makes it seem that, in spite of Wycherley's own supposed statement, *The Country Wife* was written before *The Plain Dealer*. Certainly the range of satire in the latter is broader and its sting more mordant, but its truth is less apparent and its fairness very dubious. Having already composed a first-rate comedy with satire as its basis, Wycherley went on to write an out and out satire with small regard for the amenities of Comedy and the Comic Spirit.

At Alceste we laugh, even as we ponder, but Manly is either a brute or a hero, as you choose to take him. Wycherly undoubtedly meant him for the latter and attempted to create in him a *beau ideal*. Correspondingly he debased Molière's Célimène for the sake of contrast. In comparison with the entrancing French coquette (almost surely Molière's picture of his own wife) Wycherley's Olivia is a mass of deceit and hypocrisy. She is the lady to whom Manly is engaged and with whom, on going to sea, he has left his fortune. When he returns unexpectedly, he finds her surrounded by gossiping coxcombs and flatterers, married to his best friend, and already prepared to take on a new gallant. Upon learning of these facts, he resolves to have revenge and manages to substitute himself for Olivia's new lover. Their clandestine interview is interrupted by the husband, Olivia's treachery is discovered, and she is consigned to the infamy which she so well deserves. Manly's false friend, whom she has married, also slinks away in disgrace, the Plain Dealer is satisfied, and, what is more, he gets a charming young lady to be his wife. He certainly is not worthy of Fidelia (Shakespeare's Viola, lifted bodily out of *Twelfth Night* and sent on Restoration business), but Wycherley feels that no reward is too good for this paragon of all the masculine virtues, as nothing is too bad for the underhanded Olivia. This pigeon-holing and cataloguing of characters into the "good" and the "bad" shows how far Wycherley has declined from the evenhanded justice of Molière. Yet Wycherley is the most intellectual writer of satirical comedy in English literature, and of all English dramatists he most closely approaches the serious side of the great Frenchman.

Olivia is a synthesis of social vices and, as such, is the principal object of Wycherley's animus, but there are also other characters under fire in *The Plain Dealer*. The varieties of human frailty are exemplified in Novel, who

hates imitation and doing as other people do; Lord
Plausible, who is the essence of the ceremonies that
Manly so cordially detests; Major Oldfox, a superannu-
ated fop who considers himself a poet; and the Widow
Blackacre, always involved in lawsuits. The last-named
personage, in general outlines reminiscent of the Com-
tesse in Racine's *Les Plaideurs*, is a source of much
amusement. She has a rawboned son (a rough sketch for
Tony Lumpkin), whom she is trying to bring up to the
law, and a fortune which makes her a desirable match in
the matrimonial market. Her legal propensities are
chiefly ludicrous; and in her person Wycherley attacks
the law's delays, its red tape, and its lack of justice, pro-
verbial and easy marks for a true satirist. The scene of
the whole third act is laid in Westminster Hall and
shows us Widow Blackacre embroiled with various legal
lights rejoicing in the names of Serjeant Ploddon, Mr.
Quaint, Mr. Blunder, Mr. Petulant, Mr. Buttongown,
and Mr. Splitcause. This passion for the law ultimately
leads to the Widow's ruin, as in true satire every human
weakness should do. In an effort to prove her wayward
son illegitimate she cannot refrain from employing false
witnesses, the imposture is discovered by one of her fortune-hunting suitors, and by this means he blackmails her
into a handsome settlement in lieu of matrimony. Manly
is also entangled in the Widow's legal difficulties by being the chief witness in one of her suits, so that we are
given an opportunity to hear him rail upon the evils of
the law. He is, as usual, Wycherley's mouthpiece in attacking the ills that flesh is heir to.

In fact, *The Plain Dealer* may be said to be made up
of one diatribe after another upon the conditions under
which we live, with special attention to the artificial ones

evolved by mankind. A violent attack upon human vices and a searching revelation of human shortcomings, it is a depressing, almost an indecent, play. Yet this is not surprising, for Wycherley's last comedy is avowedly a piece of satire and it is the business of satire to degrade everything that it touches; it must emphasize all that is evil in man's nature and neglect those redeeming qualities which are to be found in even the most depraved of mortals. This pattern Wycherley follows consistently and wholeheartedly throughout all his work. It begins in *Love in a Wood* with Addleplot, Dapperwit, and Alderman Gripe; it figures in *The Gentleman Dancing-Master*, though less noticeably to be sure, with Don Diego and Monsieur de Paris; it rises to the level of brilliant comedy with Pinchwife in *The Country Wife;* and it overshoots the mark into rank barbarity and loathsomeness with Olivia in *The Plain Dealer.* Each of these characters represents the excessive development of some human characteristic which Wycherley is interested in reducing to normal proportions, but it must be admitted that his zeal for reform, as expressed in the person of Manly, is itself inflated. If Pinchwife's abnormality is to be counterbalanced by a Horner, and Olivia's by a Manly, Manly, like Alceste, needs to be chastened by society. Wycherley unfortunately forgets that the satirist himself needs sometimes to be satirized.

The place of satire in literature has been much discussed; as a method of representing life on the stage it may be more open to dispute. Like it and you will like the work of William Wycherley; otherwise he is not for you to read. One always suspects that the satirist has something vicious in his own nature, else he could not understand so well and picture so vividly the objects of his scorn, but he must hold them up to ridicule in order to maintain his attitude of condemnation. A dramatist does this by putting his satirized characters into absurd situations arising directly from their moral defects; he makes them become through their own faults the victims of jokes, more or less practical in nature. So he entertains and, it may be, instructs his audience, until his indignation carries him too far. Real life is unpleasant enough, but on the stage it is especially revolting to see men and women, created in our own image, brought to ruin by an exaggeration of passions so like our own. To this human prejudice the complete satirist rarely pays much attention, but he is always most successful when he does reckon with such a natural and normal feeling. William Wycherley is at his best when he represses his universal bitterness and limits his range as in *The Country Wife;* when he lets himself be swept away to the violent extremes of *The Plain Dealer*, he loses that philosophical detachment so essential to any true expression of the Comic Spirit.

WILLIAM CONGREVE

1670—1729

THERE is an interval of more than fifteen years between the comedies of Etherege and Wycherley and those of their great successor, William Congreve. Wycherley's plays had been performed in the years from 1671 to 1676, Etherege's final work, *The Man of Mode*, in the latter year, and it was not until 1693 that Congreve's first play, *The Old Bachelor*, saw the light of day. The intervening years had been more significant from a historical than from a dramatic point of view. James II had been crowned and deposed, and William of Orange ruled in his stead; but Dryden and Shadwell still continued to dominate the theatrical world with such mediocre productions as *The Spanish Friar* and *Bury Fair*. It was no wonder then that when *The Old Bachelor* appeared upon the stage, literary London went mad over the new author. His success spurred him on to new efforts: *The Double-Dealer*, acted later in the same year, 1693; *Love for Love* of 1695; *The Mourning Bride*, his only tragedy, which need not concern us here (1697); and *The Way of the World*, which in 1700 brought Congreve's career as a playwright to an end. This last comedy, today generally considered his masterpiece, and his second one, *The Double-Dealer*, were not popular successes at the time they were produced, though they have always had the suffrages of the more intelligent. Dryden was, as usual, somewhat hyperbolic in his

praises, but he did not much overstate the case in his
verses prefixed to *The Double-Dealer:*

> In him all beauties of this age we see,
> Etherege his courtship, Southerne's purity;
> The satire, wit, and strength of manly Wycherley.

I.

It is Wycherley's influence which one notices most in
The Old Bachelor, confessedly an immature and experimental work. "How very much a boy I was when that
comedy was written; which several knew was some years
before it was acted," Congreve stated in his later life and
added, "When I wrote it I had little thoughts of the
stage, but did it to amuse myself in a slow recovery from
a fit of sickness." This may be a bit of affectation, but it
is probably not far from the truth, for *The Old Bachelor*
is much less characteristic and finished than Congreve's
other plays. To begin with, it has no less than five strands
of plot, a large number for any comedy of that age, but
particularly remarkable in the case of Congreve. Moreover, the characters are almost all reminiscent of older
plays from Captain Bluffe, a coward out of Ben Jonson,
to Heartwell, the old bachelor, himself. Heartwell, in
fact, is no other than Wycherley's Manly in the process
of formation. Manly hates all women except one, Olivia,
who deceives him and upon whom he takes revenge;
Heartwell pretends to dislike all the sex, but he secretly
loves Silvia and marries her. When he discovers that his
bride has been the mistress of one of his friends, he is in
much the same situation as is Manly when he discovers
Olivia's treachery. Manly can rally at once; Heartwell,
feeling himself tied for life, must endure the gibes of his
amused friends. Had Congreve left Heartwell married

to a whore, his satire would have been directed against the misogynist, but, like Wycherley and more modern authors, he turns the point of attack away from the individual victim upon society as a whole. Heartwell's marriage is found to have been performed by a false parson, and at the end of the play the old bachelor is left free, with a real reason for rejoicing in his liberty. The next time he will not commit himself so easily, but Manly-like he will probe the evil of woman before he gives himself into her keeping for good and all.

Wycherley's other great character, Horner, is also to be found in *The Old Bachelor*, masquerading under the name of Bellmour. His method of intrigue differs slightly from Horner's, for his way is to enjoy not only his own mistresses but those of a fickle friend, who starts many an affair that he is too bored to finish. Bellmour's principal exploit in the play is to seduce the wife of the Puritan banker, Fondlewife. Even the similarity of names shows at once that this is the story of Pinchwife, Margery, and Horner from *The Country Wife*, somewhat softened and curtailed. The Fondlewife scenes occur in only one act, the fourth, and amusing as they are, they have a very minor importance in the play as a whole. Yet Fondlewife himself is by no means an ungrateful part, as Colley Cibber once found to his great satisfaction. The jealous husband is also a parsimonious banker and a hypocritical zealot (here he links up with Alderman Gripe from *Love in a Wood*), but, if anything, he has too many traits for the brief development accorded his character. The important thing to observe is that Congreve seized on Wycherley's situation of deceiving gallant, amorous wife, and doting husband and took it over bodily in his first play. Some minor changes in detail do not affect the general tenor and outcome of the episode, which ends, as in Wycherley, with the gallant's clever lie, the wife's assent to it, and the husband's gullible belief that all has been well in his absence. It is a diverting comic situation when seen from a disinterested angle, because in it the normal social equilibrium is for a moment upset in favor of a polygamous intruder, and if the deceived husband be made odious enough, one's moral nature is unconsciously satisfied. The idea of reform inherent in even the slightest satiric implication proves sufficient justification for any lapses from propriety; and thus the spirit of laughter (which to Congreve was far more important than the spirit of righteous indignation) may be allowed full sway.

Congreve was evidently so pleased at the public's reception of this part of *The Old Bachelor* that he decided to introduce a similar situation into the sub-plots of his later plays. In the very next one, *The Double-Dealer*, it appears twice and consequently does not go so well. The position of Sir Paul Plyant is too essentially like that of Lord Froth to furnish any variety, though Congreve has taken care that in exterior details they shall not resemble one another. Sir Paul is the slave of his warm-blooded young wife, who has him swaddled in blankets at night with his hands and feet bound, and who allows him liberty only upon especial occasions. He is so completely under Lady Plyant's thumb that it is easy enough for her to coquette with whomever she pleases. It is very different in the case of the Froths. Lady Froth pretends to be devoted to her solemnly stupid husband and to her child, little Sappho, but her real interest is in poetry and learning. She is Congreve's picture of the précieuse, done with considerable understanding and no little keenness. Her literary pursuits bring her into contact with Brisk, a wit by profession, who advises her about her great poem on Lord Froth's love for his wife, to be called *The Syllabub*, "because my lord's title's Froth, egad." Much as this association with Brisk may benefit the poem technically, it seriously impairs its inspiration, for one fine day Lord Froth finds his wife in her tutor's arms and is regaled with the excuse of a dancing lesson, taken straight from Wycherley. Later they come indoors after a long time spent in star-gazing, but the imperturbable husband seems to be unconscious that star-gazing can be done in more ways than one. In *Love for Love* the interest in stars is not on the part of the lovers but on that of the husband. He is Foresight, a professional astrologer, who spends so much time over his experiments that he quite overlooks his wife's liaison with Scandal. The entire Foresight episode plays only a subordinate part in this comedy, and in Congreve's last play, *The Way of the World*, he completely omitted the by now familiar figure of an unfaithful wife. It was perhaps the failure of *The Double-Dealer*, with its Plyant-Careless and Froth-Brisk plots, which suggested to the author that he was somewhat overdoing a stock comedy situation, already sufficiently exploited and immortalized by Wycherley.

II.

There must also have been other reasons for the failure of *The Double-Dealer*. Congreve himself laid it to his use of soliloquies, to the apparent simplicity of Mellefont's character, and to the satire on vicious and affected women, but an author is a notoriously bad critic of his own work; no one of these objections, which he tries to refute in the "Epistle Dedicatory," seems to strike at the

heart of the matter. Yet a solution to this problem is extremely important for an understanding of Congreve's
work, because *The Double-Dealer* is the first of his plays
to show the characteristics of his most mature and polished writing. *The Old Bachelor* is frankly a far-off imitation of Wycherley; in his second comedy the author has
deviated from precedent and started out upon a new path
of his own. As Mr. William Archer points out in his introduction to Congreve's plays, what the dramatist is trying to do is to substitute a single story for the number of
various plots which in his time conventionally went to
make up one complete comedy. As he had himself already
sinned badly in the matter of formlessness—*The Old
Bachelor* is a hodge-podge of characters and incidents—
Congreve decided to write a play conforming to Aristotelian principles, a process which involved first of all a
simplification of material. We have his own word for his
purpose and need go no farther in search of motives. "I
made the plot as strong as I could," he said, "because it
was single; and I made it single, because I would avoid
confusion and was resolved to preserve the three unities
of the drama." His plan was certainly a commendable
one in a day of *Comical Revenges* and *Old Bachelors;*
the pity is that it was not executed as well as it was conceived.

The way in which Congreve observed the unity of
place is a striking example of his method. "Scene.—A
Gallery in Lord Touchwood's House, with Chambers adjoining." "With Chambers adjoining" relieves the se-
verely classical tone, especially as the most important
scene in the play takes place in Lady Touchwood's private apartment. In the same way, the dramatist could not
confine himself strictly to one plot and had to introduce

the Plyant and Froth stories to eke out the villainy of Maskwell. Here was an honest attempt on Congreve's part to avoid "confusion" in the drama, but he himself realized the difficulty involved. In an age accustomed to many plots and much action, it was necessary to have constant variety to divert the audience. So Congreve made the plot of *The Double-Dealer* as strong as he could because it was simple. His first problem was to seize upon a situation which would be susceptible of much elaboration, and this he found in the impediments to true love. He had already made them the basis of the most serious part of his first play: the fickle Vainlove and the modest Araminta in *The Old Bachelor* would have had no difficulties in the way of their union, had not Silvia jealously forged a letter purporting to show that Araminta was not so coy as she seemed. This simple plot, as it stood in its original form, was too lightly sketched in and too submerged by the rest of the play to produce an effect upon the audience. Still Congreve felt that it had possibilities, and he determined to make the most of them in *The Double-Dealer*. He created a pair of declared lovers, Mellefont and Cynthia; he added a more violent Silvia in the person of Lady Touchwood; and then further to complicate the situation he gave Cynthia another lover in the person of the villainous Maskwell. Maskwell's distinction was to be that his intrigues were so well concealed that he could tell them with impunity to his victims. In this way, he almost necessarily became a dominant figure, just as the wily criminal always attracts more interest than the stupid detective; and from his machinations the play takes its name.

The failure of this comedy must have been the direct result of its plan. The plot was too single and too strong for Congreve to carry it through smoothly and logically. He felt the need of variety and gained it by constantly increasing elaborations of his initial situation. The outcome is confusion worse confounded, an infinitely more perplexing imbroglio than that formed by the numerous but individually simple plots of *The Old Bachelor*. First Maskwell and Lady Touchwood must be in collaboration to embroil Mellefont with Lady Plyant; then Maskwell must try to undermine Lady Touchwood and attempt to ruin Mellefont; finally in a long and complicated last act Maskwell, disguised as Mellefont, must try to elope with Cynthia and arrange to have Lady Touchwood in Cynthia's clothes meet Mellefont at the appointed place. Needless to say, his schemes all miscarry at the last, and the lovers are happily united. How this is accomplished, really does not matter. The audience knew from the first that Maskwell's plans were too subtle to be successful and, it is to be feared, too involved to be interesting. He does things more for the sake of doing them than for any necessity inherent in the situation or in his own nature. He is the regulation villain, Iago without Iago's psychology or intellect, and as such he cannot be an object of sympathy.

On the other hand, sympathy is not preëminently demanded in a comedy, and Congreve's error at bottom may have been in trying to write a well-made play, when his temperament and talents had obviously fitted him for the more loosely knitted form of comedy. In so doing, he was attempting to put a square peg into a round hole, for comedy by its very essence has not a well-defined beginning, middle, and end; it pervades all life, it is coextensive with it, and it cannot be constrained to fit into the narrow limits of a rigidly organized art-form.

There is far more diversity of interest in Congreve's third play, *Love for Love*, and perhaps for that reason it was the most successful of all his works upon the stage. He had learned by *The Old Bachelor* not to be too diffuse, from *The Double-Dealer* not to be too concentrated; here he manages to avoid either of these extremes. His central subject is again a pair of lovers, Valentine and Angelica, but he does not confine himself to a consideration of their fate. Valentine is almost as much exercised over his debts as over his love-affair, and his feigned madness is designed to kill two birds with one stone: to extort a confession of love from Angelica, and to persuade his father to be more lenient in money matters. In neither is he successful, but his failure does not interfere with our pleasure in the play. We have all the fun of seeing Angelica outwit him and threaten to marry his father as well as of assisting at his disinheritance in favor of his sailor brother, Ben. Ben's temporary prosperity brings in new matter, for Mrs. Frail, a woman of the town, throws herself at his head, and also a marriage is arranged between him and Miss Prue, an ignorant country girl quick to learn the arts of London. This lineal descendant of Margery Pinchwife prefers the attentions of a town beau, Tattle, to those of sailor Ben, and when Ben loses his financial prospects, Mrs. Frail also deserts him. Meantime Tattle in his eagerness to marry Angelica gets tied up for life to Mrs. Frail by means of a masked marriage, Ben and Prue are left without mates, and Valentine naturally wins Angelica. It may be seen from this brief summary that the whole plot hangs together remarkably well, despite some weaknesses in its motivation and execution. One is not quite sure of what Angelica is about a good share of the time, and the marriage of Tattle and Mrs.

Frail is the height of absurdity. This device of a marriage in disguise is frequently used by Congreve—it occurs in the last act of all his first three comedies—and the fact that he so often employs it shows his dependence upon stage tricks and his paucity of real dramatic inventiveness.

The Way of the World avoids this hackneyed situation as well as the unfaithful wife motif, but it clings to Congreve's central theme, the misfortunes of lovers. Here, as in *The Double-Dealer*, the lovers' difficulties are chiefly external ones, and hence perhaps the weakness of these two plays. Unlike *Love for Love*, in which Angelica does not say "yes" until the final curtain, Cynthia and Millamant are, to all intents and purposes, plighted to Mellefont and Mirabell at the beginning of their respective comedies. The story in each case is how they get the consent and money of their elders, which are a necessity before they can be married. In *The Double-Dealer*, as we have seen, the moving force is Maskwell, the villain, who attempts to break up the match; in *The Way of the World* it is Mirabell, the hero, who is trying to get the consent of Millamant's aunt, Lady Wishfort. He has already made one bad tactical mistake by paying direct court to the old lady herself, for she has discovered what was his purpose in so doing and is now his sworn enemy. As the play begins, he is planning to substitute his servant for his uncle and to have Lady Wishfort fall in love with the impostor, incur consequent disgrace, and so work her own ruin. As a matter of fact, she does this, but meanwhile the plot has been found out by Mirabell's enemies and a countermine is sprung by the discovery of his old liaison with Mrs. Fainall, Lady Wishfort's daughter. The villains seem to be about to triumph, when Mirabell proves Fainall's own infidelity to his marriage vows, the tables are turned, and all ends happily.

The plot, it may be seen, is not very elaborate, but it is complicated. The most difficult thing is to discover the relationships of all the characters involved at the moment the curtain rises. It takes a full three acts to make clear the lay of the land, and it is not until the fourth act that Waitwell actually appears disguised as the rich uncle. By that time we know the loves and hates of Mirabell and Millamant, Lady Wishfort and Mrs. Marwood, Fainall and his wife, Sir Wilfull Witwoud, Waitwell, and Foible; but it is too tangled a skein to remember for long at a time. Fortunately the characters are not much more than puppets in their actions, and we do not greatly care what happens to them from a serious point of view. What we want to know is how Congreve incorporates the Comic Spirit with such melodramatic and mechanical plots as he uses for the background of his plays.

III.

The first thing to be considered in answering this question is the central situation in each of his comedies: a young man and a young woman in love. Congreve's constant employment of this material recalls at once the use made of it by Sir George Etherege, in whose plays, it will be remembered, the humor arose every time from an apparent disagreement between the parties in a love match. In Congreve too those scenes are always most successful where the obstacles to love are not objective but subjective, where the difference between what the lovers feel and what they say is most strongly marked; in such a case their complete social sophistication forms a striking contrast to the human promptings of their hearts. Take *The*

Old Bachelor first as an example of Congreve in embryo.
The principal lovers are Vainlove, too capricious and sentimental to be a true wooer, and Araminta, too modest
and self-conscious to be spirited game. Their one important scene together, that in which Vainlove confronts her
with the forged letter, smacks more of *comédie larmoyante* than anything else. It is unbelievably eighteenth-
century, and yet it was written before Jeremy Collier
had arisen to attack the old order. Fortunately, however,
we are not dependent upon Vainlove and Araminta for
amusement in this play; we have their friends, Bellmour
and Belinda, to herald the greater Congreve that was to
be. Bellmour even is hardly an important figure. His
place in the plot is largely to carry through his friend's
incompleted amours; it is only incidentally, as it were,
that he is in love with, and wins the hand of, the perplexing Belinda.

Belinda is a baffling character, as has been remarked by
all the critics that have considered her, probably because
Congreve started out intending to do one thing with her
and ended by doing another. She is described in the
"Dramatis Personae" as "an affected lady," and one of
Bellmour's friends tells him she is "too proud, too inconstant, too affected and too witty and too handsome for a
wife." Congreve evidently meant her as a satire on affectation, witness what he says critically of her and Miss
Prue: "I only refer those two characters to the judgment
of any impartial reader, to determine whether they are
represented so as to engage any spectator to imitate the
impudence of one, or the affectation of the other; and
whether they are not both ridiculed rather than recom-
mended." This is in reply to the censure that Jeremy Collier had found fit to bestow upon the affected manner of

Congreve's heroine, for a heroine Belinda certainly is, if to be a heroine means to have your creator lavish upon you his greatest care and put into your mouth his choicest pearls of wit and wisdom. Notice also that Bellmour has not only been told that she is "too affected" but likewise that she is "too witty," both of which characteristics make her in Congreve's mind an ideal figure for a comic heroine. In his *Essay upon Humour in Comedy*, he deliberately states that anything which appears ridiculous in a woman cannot be more than an acquired folly or affectation; and we know by his practice that he considered wit an essential ingredient of all comic writing. Small wonder then that he could not avoid showing Belinda as a dashing and charming creature, however much he may have told himself that she was receiving the righteous condemnation that she deserved.

From the beginning she loves Bellmour and he knows it, although she has never admitted it to him. " 'Tis true she is excessively foppish and affected," he says, "but in my conscience I believe the baggage loves me; for she never speaks well of me herself, nor suffers anybody else to rail at me." She pretends to fly his first approach but changes her mind at the last minute and decides to receive him. She hates his love-making, she'll not hear a sentence that begins with an "I burn" or an "I beseech you, madam," in short she will be adored in silence. Like my Lady Flippant in *Love in a Wood* and, to a lesser degree, like Lady Cockwood in *She Would if She Could*, Belinda is noted for her dislike of that "filthy, awkward, two-legged creature, man," but she can also use her tongue on her own sex. There is a whole scene which has nothing whatever to do with the plot, in which she describes in the finest spirit of satire a country family that she has met on the Exchange. The passage has often been quoted *in extenso*, but it will be enough here to notice that the two daughters were "fat as barn-door fowl; but so bedecked, you would have taken 'em for Friesland hens, with their feathers growing the wrong way." This speech is a mere *tour de force* for her wit, and she appears to far better advantage when holding Bellmour off at the same time that she wants to lead him on. She finally does accept him, capitulating grudgingly upon the surface, "O my conscience, I could find in my heart to marry thee, purely to be rid of thee," but with a deeper meaning beneath her bantering words. She knows too well the deceits of marriage to enter into it lightly, for from her mouth in this same scene comes Congreve's famous epigram, "Courtship to marriage, is as a very witty prologue to a very dull play." Certainly to hear Belinda talk of marriage makes a very witty play out of what would otherwise have been very dull dialogue.

In *The Double-Dealer* Congreve does not have so good an opportunity to show the wit of lovers. He is too occupied with his serious plot to lavish much attention on Mellefont and Cynthia. Then, too, these young people have already come to an understanding, and no contrast to their honeyed words is possible. Mellefont is contented to play the passive rôle of conventional hero, but Cynthia rather makes opportunities to display her wit. On one occasion à propos of Lord and Lady Froth she remarks that, "though marriage makes man and wife one flesh, it leaves them still two fools," and she rattles on, comparing matrimony to a game of cards or bowls. Another time she picks up Mellefont's boastfulness about his well-laid plans and demands that they be fulfilled before she marries him. She has fears that all is going too well between them, "because we are both willing; we each of us strive to reach the goal, and hinder one another in the race; I swear it never does well when the parties are so agreed." These fears are only too just from a dramatic, if not from a practical, point of view, for it is exactly this agreement of the lovers which weakens the play of Congreve's wit between them. In his next comedy, *Love for Love*, he went too far in the other direction and made his heroine's attitude a mystery both to her lover and to the audience. There can be no true comedy where the man's wooing is deadly earnest and the woman's state of mind is indecision, because in that case each takes the situation too seriously. Angelica says that she cannot come to a resolution, resolution must come to her. Then later Valentine's assumed madness stands in the way of verbal fencing, and when Angelica discovers the trick, her attempt to revenge herself on her lover is by act rather than by word. *Love for Love* has the most free and natural of Congreve's plots, and interest as to the outcome of the play is best sustained in it, but its structure hampers the witty dialogue of professed lovers, which is the finest flower of his dramatic work.

For this expression of personal feeling under the mask of polished repartee, *The Way of the World* is, by all odds, Congreve's masterpiece and Millamant his most perfect creation. She first enters escorted by Witwoud and at once reveals to the audience her contempt for him: "Dear Mr. Witwoud, truce with your similitudes; for I'm as sick of 'em—Mincing, stand between me and his wit." She is as hard on Petulant's ignorance as on Witwoud's affectations: "An illiterate man 's my aversion: I wonder at the impudence of any illiterate man to offer to make love." Her treatment of Sir Wilfull from

the country is well-nigh flawless. He has been proposed
as a match for the incomparable Millamant, and her object is to discourage him from all thoughts on that subject. She quotes Suckling to him, but of Suckling he has
never heard; she tells him that she loathes the country
and every thing pertaining to it, and he, taking heart of
grace, imagines that then they may live in town; but Millamant is still beyond him: *"Ah l'étourdi!* I hate the
town too." He is soon dismissed, without any hard feeling, and at the end of the play he helps get Lady Wishfort's consent to the marriage of Millamant and her
lover, Mirabell.

With Mirabell Millamant is on exactly the right terms
for the finest kind of comic writing. They are in love with
each other and know it, but at the time when we first see
them they are in the midst of a petty quarrel over the gay
company that Millamant insists on keeping. Mirabell is
enraged at her folly and shows no hesitancy about telling
her so, just as Manly did with Olivia, but unlike Olivia
Millamant realizes that her lover is completely in her
power. Consequently she succeeds in turning the tables on
him and in the process establishing an atmosphere of
comedy rather than of satire, for with all her love of affectations and all her social mannerisms, Millamant un-
derstands that beneath the surface man is always man
and woman still pure woman.

Mrs. Mil. Mirabell, if you persist in this offensive freedom, you'll displease me—I think I must resolve after
all, not to have you:—we shan't agree.

Mir. Not in our physic, it may be.

Mrs. Mil. And yet our distemper, in all likelihood, will
be the same; for we shall be sick of one another. I shan't

endure to be reprimanded nor instructed: 'tis so dull to act always by advice, and so tedious to be told of one's faults—I can't bear it. Well, I won't have you, Mirabell —I'm resolved—I think—you may go.—Ha! ha! ha! what would you give, that you could help loving me?

Mir. I would give something that you did not know I could not help it.

Mrs. Mil. Come, don't look grave then. Well, what do you say to me?

She goes on laughing at him in this fashion whenever they meet, until in the fourth act she decides to take him. She lays down long conditions as to the way they shall live after marriage and then gives him a chance to do the same thing in a milder way. So each rails at the married habits of the opposite sex in quite the most brilliant and masterly scene in all Congreve's theatre. They are like Benedick and Beatrice, but with less humanity than Shakespeare would ever have allowed his characters; they are like Dorimant and Harriet Woodvil, but with sharper tongues and keener brains than Etherege could ever have conceived of. Their encounters mark the highest point reached in the English Comedy of Manners as far as dialogue is concerned, and yet theirs is not quite dialogue purely for the sake of dialogue. Millamant loves her admirer, but it is hard for her to admit that she has been in the wrong. Her wit protects her as long as it can, but Mirabell is equal to the situation and presses her hard at every instant. Perhaps though he would never have completely subdued her, had not a third party come to join them and so break the tension. This is no less a person than Mrs. Fainall, Mirabell's past mistress but his present well-wisher. Millamant appeals to her.

Mrs. Mil. Fainall, what shall I do? Shall I have him? I think I must have him.

Mrs. Fain. Ay, ay, take him, take him what should you do?

Mrs. Mil. Well then—I'll take my death I'm in a horrid fright—Fainall, I shall never say it—well—I think—I'll endure you.

Mrs. Fain. Fy! fy! have him, have him, and tell him so in plain terms: for I am sure you have a mind to him.

Mrs. Mil. Are you? I think I have—and the horrid man looks as if he thought so too—well, you ridiculous thing you, I'll have you—I won't be kissed, nor I won't be thanked—here kiss my hand though.—So, hold your tongue now, don't say a word.

In such fashion is the peerless Millamant wooed and won, half way between grave and gay, seriousness and jest, naturalness and sophistication, hardly ever without some overtone of deeper meaning and never at all with any touch of heaviness. It is a splendid example of artificial comedy at its most perfect—polished and subtle, but necessarily limited in scope.

IV.

It is easy to see that, if only one situation furnishes such opportunity for wit and if that situation can only be carried off successfully in one out of four plays, the comic dramatist, like Congreve, is cribbed and confined in his use of material. Once or twice in his career he may stumble on exactly that arrangement of characters and episodes which will give most opportunity to his genius, but for the greater share of the time he must be content with the second-rate. However, a real wit is never at a

loss to show his brilliance, and in all Congreve's writing
the dialogue cracks and scintillates, whether there be any
real occasion for it or not. This is not so true in *The Old
Bachelor*, the least typical of his plays, but even here we
have Belinda engaged in set pieces of description purely
to display her wit. In one significant passage she has met
Mr. Sharper in St. James's Park and wishes to get him
out of the way that Vainlove and Araminta may have a
tête-à-tête. "Come, Mr. Sharper," she says, "you and I
will take a turn and laugh at the vulgar; both the great
vulgar and the small. . . . Oh Lord, walk this way! I
see a couple, I'll give you their history." At this point
they disappear, and when they enter in the next scene,
we get just the tag end of the same conversation:

Belin. Nay, we have spared nobody, I swear. Mr.
Sharper, you're a pure man; where did you get this excellent talent of railing?

Sharp. Faith, madam, the talent was born with me:—I
confess, I have taken care to improve it, to qualify me
for the society of ladies.

That is all, but it is extremely revealing. Mere conversation, especially of a cutting and slanderous kind, is occu-
pying Congreve's thoughts, though so far his characters
are only allowed to indulge in it while they are off the
stage.

In *The Double-Dealer* with his new approach to plot
and structure, we find also a new attitude to wit. The
complicated thread of this play makes almost no demand
for cleverness in conversation; so Congreve injects it
wherever he can find room. Brisk, for example, is a professional wit, and every time he appears upon the stage it is
to shower epigrams on the company. At his entrance in

the first scene he holds up the exposition for a whole page while he discourses on leaving company and coming into it, and he figures largely in the second scene of the play, which is entirely given over to plotless conversation. The subject of this discussion between all the men in the cast except Maskwell, who is held in reserve for more serious business, is "wit," which Lord Froth solemnly tries to suppress at every opportunity. He goes to the playhouse whenever he can, on purpose not to laugh at the poet's jests. " 'Tis true it makes against wit," comments Brisk, "and I'm sorry for some friends of mine that write, but, egad, I love to be malicious. Nay, deuce take me, there's wit in't too; and wit must be foiled by wit; cut a diamond with a diamond; no other way, egad!" This is, of course, false wit in the sense that it is artificial and labored, but it is the false wit possible only to a Congreve, the false wit which forms the backbone of a comedy of manners. Careless, a true wit, may be successful in putting Brisk in his place, but it is Brisk's brilliant attack that stimulates his rivals, and the audience, to follow his lead in a less vivid and so in a more natural way.

As the play progresses, especially one with such an involved and elaborate story as *The Double-Dealer*, the wit naturally takes a subordinate place. There is too much plotting and counterplotting to allow time for mere verbal fencing, but in the third act Congreve stops again for an interlude. Like the Sharper-Belinda talk in *The Old Bachelor*, it is about scandal, always a provocative subject for set wit as well as for satire. Wycherley used it most artfully for the latter purpose in his picture of Olivia's salon in *The Plain Dealer;* Congreve is here employing it for no other reason than to amuse. Sheridan has told us, once and for all, that the malice in a clever saying is the barb which makes it stick, but Congreve had already discovered this truth if he had not exactly formulated it. Sir Paul Plyant is much entertained by my Lady Whifler, Mr. Sneer, Sir Laurence Loud, and "that gang," whom Lord Froth and Cynthia find to be quite insupportable. Consequently the two latter, with the help of Lady Froth and Brisk, lay themselves out to criticize all the persons of their acquaintance. Cynthia, to be sure, is somewhat ashamed of doing so, but unlike Sheridan's Maria she dissembles her feelings enough to join in the general display of wit and ill-nature. This scene does not last long, for, as in the case of Lady Wishfort's cabal-nights in *The Way of the World*, Congreve's overelaborate plot soon drives out the mere photographic study of manners in which he so excelled. It is always a cause for regret when an author's talents in one direction come into conflict with his limitations in another; certainly Congreve's plays, like those of Shaw in our own time, often suffer from having their pointed and literary dialogue surrounded by a complicated and inferior intrigue.

His last two comedies are not quite so obviously torn between wit and plot, because *Love for Love* contains a clear and interesting story and in *The Way of the World* wit rules supreme. Not that *Love for Love* is without sparkling talk, for its whole first act is merely preparatory to the action and gives a splendid chance for all the characters to converse. Besides the hero, Valentine, and his railing friend, Scandal, the clever sayings fall chiefly to the share of Jeremy, an incredibly brilliant servant, and to Tattle, another of Congreve's fools, of whom Pope asks if they be fools indeed. Scandal's description of Tattle shows the characters of both men and also is an admirable example of the author's style at its most finished: "The rogue will speak aloud in the posture of a whisper; and deny a woman's name, while he gives you the marks of her person: he will forswear receiving a letter from her, and at the same time show you her hand in the superscription. . . . In short, he is a public professor of secrecy, and makes proclamation that he holds private intelligence." This last epigram is in Congreve's best manner; every word in it tells, and the ring of the whole sentence, labored and elaborate as it is, strikes the ear as with the cadence of preordained harmonies. The antithesis of "public professor" and "proclamation" to "secrecy" and "private intelligence" proclaims a perfect sense of paradox—and of balance. Another important wit scene in this play is the quartet in the third act between Tattle, Valentine, Scandal, and Angelica on the secrecy of men and the chastity of women. For some five pages this theme is developed by question and answer, after which Congreve's cynical conclusion is concentrated into the concluding couplet of a song:

> He alone won't betray in whom none will confide:
> And the nymph may be chaste that has never been tried.

Love for Love is essentially an acting play with an intelligible plot and the wit subordinate to it. *The Way of the World*, Congreve's literary masterpiece, was a failure on the stage and deserved to be. An audience cannot be expected to sit with any pleasure through five acts of drama (particularly an abstruse fifth one), if there be no coherent plot to hold one's interest and, in fact, no attraction but enchanting dialogue. After all, a play is to be acted on a stage before an audience and must be written with that end in view; it is unlike purer forms of literature which fulfill every requirement if they can be read with pleasure in the solitude of one's study. Judged by this standard, Congreve's last and most characteristic play is not a play at all, but a so-called "closet drama," written in well-nigh perfect dialogue, which must be read and reread to be appreciated. Moreover, this finished style pervades the entire comedy. One has only to open it at random to light on some gem of comic insight polished to a fine lustre of expression. Mirabell tells Fainall that his mistress's failings have become as familiar to him as his own; and in all probability he will soon like them as well. To which the worldly Fainall's answer is: "Marry her, marry her! be half as well acquainted with her charms, as you are with her defects, and my life on't, you are your own man again." Witwoud has a *mot* on friendship, which, he says, is as dull without freedom "as love without enjoyment, or wine without toasting." Petulant asserts that women should "show their innocence by not understanding what they hear, or else show their discretion by not hearing what they would not be thought to understand." Even a waiting-maid at a chocolate-house, when asked what time her clock says cannot reply without a jocular, "Turned of the last canonical hour, sir." All these quotations are from the first act of the play, and as yet the resplendent Millamant has not appeared upon the stage. When she does, as we have already seen, her creator's genius reaches the highest point to which it ever attains.

V.

For better or worse Congreve's distinction as an author rests on his ability to write witty dialogue in literary form. The satirical spirit which he inherited from Wycherley and with which he began his dramatic writing was foreign to his nature and could not long monopolize his art. He might give us a Manly (Heartwell) and a Horner (Bellmour) in his earliest play, but as soon as he created a character, like Belinda, whose failing was affected wit, he turned instinctively from condemnation to sympathy. Wit was really his be-all and his end-all, the chief object of his existence and his writing. In all his last three comedies he gives us an affected wit, Brisk, Tattle, and Witwoud; two true wits, Mellefont and Careless, Valentine and Scandal, Mirabell and Fainall; and above all a heroine who outshines all the men, Cynthia, Angelica, and Millamant. This girl, always acted by Congreve's idol, Mrs. Bracegirdle, constantly triumphs over those about her and at the end of the play appears resplendent, the cynosure of all eyes. If she has some reason to mock her lover, as Cynthia does not, and yet if, unlike Angelica, she acknowledges that she is in love, the perfect comic situation is achieved. Congreve has evolved such a relationship in the conflict of Mirabell and Millamant, dressed it in all the cleverness at his command, and given us in the scenes between them not only first-rate literary writing, but a splendid example of comedy in its most refined form. Moreover, for a moment he has captured the essence of drama.

This is all the more striking because, for the most part, his plays are so artificial and unreal. Beginning with the diffuseness of *The Old Bachelor* and going on to the concentrated intrigues of *The Double-Dealer*, Congreve is essentially an author who does not know how to write for the stage. In *Love for Love* he seems to be struggling towards a true appreciation of the playwright's art—in spite of his failure to make clear Angelica's character and motives—but in *The Way of the World* he has relapsed again into dramatic chaos. He did not, he could not, see life from the emotional angle for more than a moment at a time, perhaps because he saw it so keenly from the comic point of view. To such a dispassionate spectator of the *comédie humaine*, the world is an absurdly tangled mass of folly without head or tail, beginning or end. He cannot see it, or any part of it, as an artistic whole but must content himself with laughing for a moment and passing on to view ever fresh absurdities, unless he be a Molière and ever holds fast the just proportion between deadly earnest and the lightest rapier stroke. If he attempts to perform that difficult feat, he may err in the direction of too great savagery, as Wycherley did; or, on the other hand, he may, like Congreve, provoke the idle laugh.

"Wit is at the best but the sign to good understanding," wrote Congreve himself in his reply to Collier, "it is hung out to recommend the entertainment which may be found within; and it is very well when the invitation can be made good." So our author stands self-condemned. His work has the excellent sauce of wit, but it lacks the body of good understanding. The surface is so dazzling that sometimes one forgets what is lacking beneath it, till, upon reflection, it is only too evident that Congreve never really understood the fundamental principles of human behavior. He skimmed lightly over the appearances of life but never stopped to question himself as to their whys and wherefores. He is, after all, only a professional funny man, though it must be granted that the entertainment he offers us is of the most rarefied and intricate kind. His plays may seldom be seen upon the boards, but they will always be read by connoisseurs, who know that he stands unrivaled in English letters for the

brilliant and sparkling wit with which he clothes a superficial attitude towards the world. However limited and
unreliable William Congreve's work may be, it is the supreme expression in our literature of a very special and a
very conspicuous phase of the Comic Spirit.

SIR JOHN VANBRUGH
1664—1726

THE dramatic work of Sir John Vanbrugh is by no means so easy to treat *en masse* as is that of Etherege, Wycherley, or Congreve. Each of these earlier authors wrote three or four comedies definitely his own in conception and execution, relying little upon outside aid or inspiration; an analysis of their acknowledged plays furnishes a definite gauge by which to judge their aims and their accomplishment. It is otherwise with Vanbrugh. In exactly how many plays he had a hand is still a matter of dispute, but we are practically certain that we do not today possess all of his writing for the stage. Even some of the work which is admittedly his has strong affiliations with that of other men; several of his plays are no more than translations, and the most famous of them all owes its genesis to another comedy of the day. In January, 1696, Colley Cibber had made his first bid for public favor as a playwright with the phenomenally successful *Love's Last Shift; or, The Fool in Fashion*, to which Vanbrugh was inspired to write a sequel known as *The Relapse; or, Virtue in Danger*. It was produced in December of the same year and followed in the spring of 1697 by Vanbrugh's only other complete and original play, *The Provok'd Wife*. These two comedies, together with the fragmentary *A Journey to London*, left unfinished at his death, are the most important literary productions of their author. They are entirely his own work, and upon them his reputation as a comic dramatist must ultimately stand or fall.

There must also be noticed the numerous translations and adaptations with which he was at one time or another concerned. Of these the most successful is *The Confederacy*, performed in 1705, a highly amusing version of Dancourt's *Les Bourgeoises à la Mode* and a great improvement upon its original. Vanbrugh's other more pretentious translations are: *Aesop* (1696-1697) from Boursault's *Les Fables d'Ésope* (with a brief unfinished Second Part never acted); *The False Friend* (1702) from Le Sage's *Le Traître Puni*, which in turn comes from a Spanish source; and *The Mistake* (1705) from Molière's *Dépit Amoureux*. His lesser productions, which are practically negligible in estimating the value of his work, may be recorded here for the sake of completeness: *The Pilgrim* (1700), a prose alteration of Fletcher's romantic comedy of the same name; *The Country House* (date unknown), from Dancourt's *La Maison de Campagne;* *Squire Trelooby* (1704), in collaboration with Congreve and Walsh from Molière's *Monsieur de Pourceaugnac;* and perhaps—though Vanbrugh's authorship of the work is uncertain—a version of Molière's *Sganarelle; ou, Le Cocu Imaginaire*, entitled *The Cuckold in Conceit* (1707). The last-named play was never published, and it is also doubtful whether or not the extant version of *Monsieur de Pourceaugnac* is that in which Vanbrugh had a part. Thus it can be seen that, though there are no less than eleven plays with which the name of this busy soldier and architect is connected, only seven of the eleven have any intrinsic value in themselves. Of these seven, three are distinctly second-rate, so that we are thrown back upon *The Confederacy* and Vanbrugh's three original plays for a discussion of his place in the history of English comedy. On these four works his position depends; with them one must primarily deal in studying their author.

I.

Unlike the other comic dramatists already discussed, who began by experimentation and only gradually arrived at their best work, Vanbrugh started his career as a playwright with his masterpiece, *The Relapse*. The circumstances of its composition are of the first importance in understanding its author's attitude towards his art. Colley Cibber had just obtained an enormous success with his *Love's Last Shift*, a play which has the distinction of being the first real sentimental comedy in English. It is the story of Loveless, a rake, who in the last act is made to see the error of his ways by his faithful wife, Amanda; "and so they lived happily ever after," is Cibber's way of dismissing his characters at the end of the play. The town applauded heartily, but the more intelligent stopped to consider. "The end of a comedy is the beginning of a tragedy;" yes, but if one is less disturbed at marital infidelity than amused at the incongruity of a husband's protestations and his actions, the dictum should be altered to read: "The end of a sentimental comedy is but the beginning of a true comedy." At least, such was Vanbrugh's view. It was all very well for Loveless to swear eternal constancy in the fifth act, but what if he should swear it in the first act? In *The Relapse* he does so, but business calls him from the country to London; he sees Berinthia, a young widow at the play; she turns out to be his wife's cousin; and Amanda insists upon having her come to live with them. Berinthia is soon found to be a

person of easy morals, and Loveless's inevitable relapse
sets in. He hides in Berinthia's closet, discloses himself
at the psychological moment, and bears off Berinthia,
who all the time is protesting *very softly:* "Help! help!
I'm ravished! ruined! undone! O Lord, I shall never be
able to bear it." The contrast between Berinthia's words
and her feelings and that between Loveless's past promises and present deeds provide a high comedy scene of the
first water. Vanbrugh here achieved a philosophical detachment and an intellectual judgment in regard to the
affairs of this world which insured him of power and
ability as a comic writer. Unfortunately he could not
maintain the nice balance he had here hit upon, and never
again was he quite so successful in the realm of thoughtful laughter.

He was too kindly to be continually occupied with such
bitter mirth, nor did he have the courage of his convictions, either moral or artistic. *Love's Last Shift* had been
a financial success, and it had won the approval of the
more serious-minded element in the public. How could
one fly in the face of such a marked preference for the
improving at the expense of the amusing? Vanbrugh had
the comic sense to see the absurdity of eleventh-hour re-
pentances, but not the strength of character necessary to
keep from giving the public what it wanted. Therefore
as a pendant to Loveless's *Relapse*, we have in the very
same play the companion picture of Amanda's *Virtue in
Danger.* Just as Loveless meets his Berinthia, so Amanda
meets her Worthy, and her situation is the more difficult
because Worthy is trying, by foul means as well as fair,
to bring about her surrender. He almost succeeds in ac-
complishing his purpose, but at the crucial moment
Amanda breaks from him with the cry, "Then save me,

virtue, and the glory's thine," Worthy repents, sentiment prevails, and the Comic Spirit is utterly routed. This strand of the plot is not at all important from the point of view of laughter—many of the scenes in which Amanda figures are written in an attempt at blank verse, a form essentially hostile to the presence of the Comic Spirit—but it is extremely significant as a contrast with, and a commentary upon, the Loveless-Berinthia episode. It is with the more sophisticated prose story that Vanbrugh's heart lay (notice that *Virtue in Danger* is but the sub-title of the play), though of course in answering the criticisms of Jeremy Collier he played up the moral part of his comedy, because he did not have the necessary force to stand by his convictions. He was essentially a comic dramatist with the comic attitude towards life; by compromising with public taste he produced a great deal of very mediocre work, strongly tinged with the taint of sentimentality. Take, for instance, *The False Friend*, in which the character of Leonora, the heroine, is made even more noble and pure than it was in Le Sage and his Spanish source.

Vanbrugh's second play in order of merit as well as of original composition shows the same weakness. *The Provok'd Wife* also deals with a threatened disruption of marriage bonds, but here instead of two plots, a sentimental one for the wife and a comic one for the husband, our interest is centered in a story which combines both of these elements in itself. Sir John and Lady Brute are a badly matched couple, it is true: he married her from physical desire only, and she accepted him to gain money and position. It was not likely that theirs would prove a happy union, nor is one surprised to find that Sir John's good-natured bestiality is driving his wife to seek revenge and a gallant. She arranges an anonymous rendezvous with Constant in Spring-Garden, where her husband's arrival makes it necessary for her to reveal her identity to her lover. Constant seizes his opportunity and violently presses his case, until he is just about to force the lady into a convenient arbor. She is meantime protesting, halfway between serious like Amanda and feigning like Berinthia, when their tête-à-tête is interrupted by two eavesdroppers who have been hiding in the arbor during the entire interview. This scene occurs in the fourth act, and one hopes for a resolution of the love interest in the remainder of the play, but instead of carrying out the motif of Constant's affair with Lady Brute, Vanbrugh turns his attention to the husband's attitude towards these proceedings. Sir John is informed of what has occurred but is too cowardly to take any action about it; the matter is hushed up, and so the play ends. Vanbrugh has clearly shirked working out to its logical conclusion the situation that he had here created: he was afraid of the relentless outcome demanded by comedy, though he cannot be said to have definitely falsified the issue. Lady Brute shows no Amanda-like repentance, and as Sir John seems too craven to interfere further in his wife's affairs, one would infer that the intrigue with Constant was to be continued and completed a little later. Yet this is left to the imaginations of the audience, and Vanbrugh could say to Jeremy Collier with some show of truth: "Poor Constant . . . he has not got even his mistress yet; he had not, at least, when the play was last acted."

Perhaps it was this desire for an incompleted intrigue which suggested to Vanbrugh the translation of Dancourt's comedy, *Les Bourgeoises à la Mode*. At any rate, *The Confederacy* is his most successful adaptation, and it contains a double version of the plot to which we have already found him so partial. Clarissa and Araminta (to use Vanbrugh's names for the characters), wives of two rich city scriveners, are tired of their unfashionable avaricious husbands and plan together to get money from other admirers. The quirk in the plot comes from the fact that each has an affair with the other's husband and is successful in bleeding her victim in return for a promise of future favors. Before these promises come due, the cross-intrigue is discovered by the husbands, and the *status quo ante* is reëstablished (except that the designing women have made a considerable financial gain by their transactions). Vanbrugh ends his version of the story with a dialogue between the wives which explains once more how much he desired to see life from the unmoral point of view, but how convention came thrusting itself in to spoil his best-laid plans:

> *Aram.* And I suppose for us, Clarissa, we are to go on with our dears, as we used to do.
> *Clar.* Just in the same tract, for this late treaty of agreement with 'em was so unnatural you see it could not hold.

The false ending is not obtrusively felt here, as the situation is so artificial as to be incredible, but it is worth noticing that, although he hints at renewed complications, Vanbrugh ends his play with a formal renunciation of further mischief by the wives; in the original, Dancourt thought it unnecessary to do more than complete the essentially comic plot in the spirit in which it had been begun and conducted throughout.

Vanbrugh himself never finished the double plot in his fragmentary *A Journey to London*, so that we cannot be sure whether comedy or sentiment would have prevailed in his last play. Perhaps, as in his first one, the honors would have been evenly divided. We are told by Colley Cibber, who revised and completed this comedy under the title of *The Provok'd Husband*, that Lady Arabella was ultimately to have been turned out of doors by her husband. This seems quite probable, as it would involve no necessary infidelity in marriage, which evidently Vanbrugh wished particularly to avoid. Lady Arabella is vain, selfish, and extravagant, but she has no lover and is considering none; hence the proprieties could be maintained, even though she should be driven from home. Cibber, of course, is more charitable and gives Lady Arabella a fifth act repentance, which removes from the play all the strength he himself so much admired in Vanbrugh's original. Cibber also preserves the chastity of Lady Headpiece, who has come up from the country with her husband to taste the pleasures of the town. What Vanbrugh would have done with this, his main plot, is open to question, but one fears the artistic worst. True, as the play stands in its unfinished condition, a heavy assault is being directed against Lady Headpiece, but it is quite likely that her honor would ultimately have been preserved. Never after the Loveless-Berinthia scene did Vanbrugh again dare to paint the facts of life as he humorously saw them; it would have been surprising indeed if his comic sense had reinstated itself at the end of his life and had once more carried off the victory. Meanwhile we have *A Journey to London*, as its author left it, with all its dash and brilliance, and we need not inquire too curiously how the plot might have been weakened by completion. It is enough to sit in admiration before Vanbrugh's depiction of dissolute London society and its effect upon a simple-minded family from the country.

II.

Country folk seem to have had an especial attraction for our author, for even in his first play, *The Relapse*, some of the best scenes are those laid at the country-house of Sir Tunbelly Clumsey—the first time in an important Restoration Comedy that the painter of contemporary manners had been willing to turn his attention from the foibles of fashionable society and fasten it upon the life of the provinces. Vanbrugh himself did not perhaps realize the far-reaching significance of his innovation. As the range of comedy widened and its narrow boundaries were pushed back, it became harder and harder for the dramatist to maintain the clarity of vision and the fixity of purpose with which he had been wont to regard his material. Vanbrugh is, no doubt, more human in his outlook than Congreve, his atmosphere is fresher and more natural, but by the same token his feelings sometimes interfere with the comic sense of detachment necessary to his art. He has probed beneath the surface of things, as Congreve never did, but in so doing he has forfeited many an honest laugh for the sake of a kindly and sympathetic, and sometimes even an emotionally false, touch of nature. "Brother Van" was Vanbrugh's nickname, and how can a brotherly man be expected to laugh whole-heartedly at his fellow men? As a matter of fact, Vanbrugh does laugh at them a great deal, but it is difficult for him to make a genial, simple, and straightforward person like Sir Tunbelly Clumsey appear continuously ridiculous. Sir Tunbelly's rough-and-ready exterior is amusing, so is his armed defense of his home, so is his primitive management of his daughter; but, after all, he loves Hoyden at bottom, and she treats him badly. When he hears of her secret marriage, he cannot console himself with vain sophistry as Lord Foppington does, his indignation will not be quelled, and he tears out of the room, shouting to Hoyden's husband: "Art thou brother to that noble peer? —Why, then, that noble peer, and thee, and thy wife, and the nurse, and the priest—may all go and be damned together." This situation is quite natural, it must be admitted, but it is too poignant to be genuinely comic; in it the emotions of life come too near us to allow us to be thoroughly amused at Sir Tunbelly's sad plight.

Such was Vanbrugh's danger in widening the canvas of comedy, but it was a danger at first but little appreciated. The more obvious result of this innovation was to give the dramatist an opportunity to paint new types. Sir Tunbelly himself was a novelty and, on the whole, a humorous one. His sleek, pleasure-loving chaplain and the family nurse are also the source of much merriment. Best of all is Miss Hoyden, Sir Tunbelly's daughter. She is Vanbrugh's version of Wycherley's Margery Pinchwife and Congreve's Prue, but we have the great advantage of seeing Hoyden on her native heath, far from London's bustle and roar. The breath of out of doors that we get with her appearance gives her a vitality and reality quite foreign to the artificial atmosphere surrounding her forerunners. We first hear of her being locked up before the gate of the house can be opened to a strange man, and then we see the effect of such treatment upon her. "Sure never nobody was used as I am," she says on her introduction to the audience. "I know well enough what other girls do, for all they think to make a fool of me. It's well I have a husband coming, or, ecod, I'd marry the baker, I would so! Nobody can knock at the gate, but presently I must be locked up; and here's the young greyhound bitch can run loose about the house all day long, she can; 'tis very well." This speech gives us all of Hoyden: her sophistication, her determination to marry, her unwillingness to be kept in subjection, her free and easy tongue, above all, her intense breeziness, which sweeps all obstacles before it and finally secures for her exactly what she wants in this world, liberty and a husband. It is a masterly picture held in almost perfect solution between the serious and the amusing, nature and artificial comedy. No wonder that Vanbrugh drew her again on a smaller scale in Corinna, the bourgeois daughter of *The Confederacy*, and in Miss Betty Headpiece, the pert country miss come up to town in *A Journey to London*.

Another rather notable instance of our author's predilection for rural types appears in his additions to Boursault's *Les Fables d'Ésope*. His single new character among those who come to Aesop for redress is Polidorus Hogstye, a country gentleman, who appears in the fourth act with complaints against the system of taxation. He would like to avoid paying all taxes, because they make such a drain upon his personal finances, and one supposes that Sir Tunbelly Clumsey would most heartily have agreed with him. Again, in the brief Second Part of *Aesop*, Aesop talks with another country gentleman, who feels that he and his family could run the government far better than is now being done. This scene is reminiscent of that between Ésope and Cléon in Boursault's second Aesop play, *Ésope à la Cour*, but the important point is that Vanbrugh turns Cléon into a country personage merely for the sake of drawing one more rural type. Another significant change made by the Englishman is to have this countryman convinced by Aesop of the error of his ways, though Cléon more amusingly remains obstinate and firm in his convictions, even after Ésope's lecture to him.

Vanbrugh pictured a country gentleman for the last time in *A Journey to London*. Sir Francis Headpiece has left his home at Headpiece Hall to come up to the metropolis as member of parliament for the ancient borough of Gobble-guinea. These facts speak for themselves and show, at once, that with a change of scene from the country to the town, sympathy for the characters must inevitably give way to satire upon them. Sir Francis is ambitious to be famous and popular, he is grasping and avaricious; his wife (like the bourgeois Clarissa in *The Confederacy*) wants to ape the ways—and finances—of the fine ladies of fashion; his son, a dull, lubberly sort of whelp, too stupid to know what he wants, is fascinated by the first pretty girl he sees; his daughter, pert and forward, thinks only of her shape, her clothes, and prospective suitors. This entire family is depicted in the dry light of remorseless comedy, yet without the bitter and misanthropic sting which Wycherley put into all his satirical portraits. The brotherly Vanbrugh could afford to laugh in a kindly way at his Sir Tunbellys and Sir Francises, his Miss Hoydens and Miss Bettys, realizing very well that they all were worthy persons at bottom and that in the proper environment they would all be respectable members of society. When Cibber at the end of *The Provok'd Husband* dismisses the Headpieces to the country again, one has only the most charitable and optimistic feelings for them, although it is to be remembered that Cibber was always willing to express in full the nobility which Vanbrugh was satisfied with implying. How their original creator would finally have treated the Head-pieces we can never know; perhaps it is as well for all concerned that their history was never authoritatively finished. Comedy is in its essence a transitory, fleeting thing, which may be destroyed by attempting to relate it too closely to the serious events of life. Certainly many of the finest comic figures in our literature are, like the Headpieces, creatures who *are* rather than who *do*.

III.

This static quality is distinctly noticeable in Vanbrugh's single most famous character: Lord Foppington. In him our author's comic genius burst forth and flowered into full perfection. Foppington was not a new character upon the Restoration stage, but in drawing him Van-brugh revealed a finish and a power which make this por-traiture unique. The type had already been definitely fixed in Etherege's Sir Fopling Flutter and Cibber's Sir Novelty Fashion; in fact, Vanbrugh dared to take Cib-ber's very character from *Love's Last Shift* and continue his part in *The Relapse*. The glory in such a case always remains with him who best accomplishes his task, and there can be no doubt of Lord Foppington's title to pre-eminence among all the beaux of English comedy. From the moment when we first see him being dressed by his valet and criticizing the work of various tradesmen till his last courtly surrender of Hoyden, one is the complete thrall of his polished personality. After all this man is no mere fool, he realizes quite well what he is about, and if that fact makes him the more reprehensible, it also makes him the more delightful; he fully appreciates how absurd he is, but his absurdity is the price of his pleasure. "Thinking to me is the greatest fatigue in the world,"

"To mind the inside of a book, is to entertain one's self with the forced product of another man's brain," "My life, madam, is a perpetual stream of pleasure, that glides through such a variety of entertainments, I believe the wisest of our ancestors never had the least conception of any of 'em:" such are Lord Foppington's mottoes, and he goes on to elaborate upon how he passes every hour of the precious twenty-four. Later in rewriting a part of *The Provok'd Wife*, Vanbrugh undertook to give a companion picture of how the lady of fashion spends her day, but he was not able to recapture the first fine, careless buoyancy of Lord Foppington's tirade.

Lord Foppington *is*, he exists, but more than that he is exactly the sort of a person fitted to be the dominant figure in a comedy. Gifted with brains, intelligence, and charm, he is willing to live upon the surface of life, a gorgeous butterfly flitting from flower to flower. He is not an important member of society, economically considered, but he is an ornament to it, without whom the world would be a less interesting place. He is the very embodied essence of that comedy which cannot probe into the dark depths of human existence, but which is a practical necessity for the daily business of living. The more serious-minded an individual is, the greater his need for this safety valve of humor; and hence the purpose and function of "thoughtful laughter." Inasmuch as this kind of comedy is by its nature an intangible, momentary affair, we are not surprised to see Lord Foppington take no very important part in the serious plot of the play. He is, of course, a character that does not develop and his sole function, structurally considered, is to unite the two plots of *The Relapse*. He attempts to make love to Amanda, the virtuous wife, and is wounded by Loveless for his

pains; he refuses to give £500 to his brother and so drives
the poverty-stricken rascal to impose upon Sir Tunbelly
Clumsey and Miss Hoyden. Quite naturally Foppington's importance decreases as the complications in the
plot arise, for when action occurs any purely satiric character must inevitably be set aside. His confinement to the
dog-kennel has not the same comic value as his scintillat-
ing wit, and in the fifth act he barely appears until the
dénouement. He is struck dumb by the news of Hoyden's
marriage to another but recovers himself sufficiently to
consider what is the best course for a man of fashion to
pursue under the circumstances: "Now, for my part, I
think the wisest thing a man can do with an aching heart
is to put on a serene countenance; for a philosophical air
is the most becoming thing in the world to the face of a
person of quality." So we leave him, his comic view of
life still triumphing over all odds, as he assures us com-
placently in the Epilogue that,

> Good clothes are things
> Have ever been of great support to kings.

What would Shakespeare or Swift or Carlyle have said
to such a superficial view of the clothes philosophy?

Superficial the fop essentially is, and as such he seems
to have had an especial appeal for Vanbrugh's imagination. In working over Boursault's Aesop story, he introduced into the last act Aesop's appearance as a gentleman
of fashion in a gay foppish dress, a long peruke, etc.
Dramatically this disguise serves to contrast with Aesop's
inner nobility, which is so soon to assert itself, but practically it was probably suggested by the fact that Colley
Cibber, who had created and made famous the part of
Foppington, was also the stage representative of Aesop;

and both the actor and the audience would be delighted
at this new opportunity for a favorite performer to appear in a favorite rôle. Again in the unacted Second Part
of *Aesop*, Vanbrugh introduced a dude called Empty,
who describes his ordinary occupations day by day and
asks Aesop for his daughter's hand. This fine fellow
thinks that any girl would be only too glad to marry him
and remains constant in his opinion, even after Aesop's
attempts to disillusionize him. Empty is only roughly
sketched in by Vanbrugh, but the ease and skill with
which the dramatist did such incidental figures is an evidence of the interest which he took in the mere exterior of
social life.

The female of this species is represented by Lady
Fancyful out of *The Provok'd Wife*. We are introduced
to her as she sits before her mirror at her morning toilet,
attended by a flattering French maid, known as "Mademoiselle," and a candid English one, whose lack of tact
soon causes her mistress to drive her from the room. Mademoiselle is the Lady's real confidante, and to her she confesses grave secrets. All the town is in love with her, but
she will not hearken to them. "And yet I could love; nay,
fondly love, were it possible to have a thing made on purpose for him; for I'm not cruel, Mademoiselle; I'm only
nice." However, when one ambitious spark dares to criticize her openly for vanity and affectation, Fancyful takes
a decided interest in him. For a long time she cannot
make up her mind whether to write to him or not, but finally decides against it after a most amusing scene of in-
determination. Another of her weaknesses is for poetry
and music. She writes verses sometimes, and sometimes
she herself sings—"Chevy Chase" for instance, much to
the admiration of every one about her. To be sure, it is

from her own mouth that we hear of her success, but that is not surprising. Fancyful is a female counterpart of Foppington, and in both cases it is what these characters think of themselves that forms the humorous contrast to what other people think of them and what they really are. The lady is not so complete a portrait as Foppington, but she does very well as a companion piece to, and commentary upon, Vanbrugh's greatest comedy creation.

IV.

Fancyful also provides an essential part of the intrigue in *The Provok'd Wife*. Although she has decided not to write to Heartfree, her critic, she does clearly show her partiality for him and in this way provokes the spirited Belinda to rivalry. Belinda decides to fascinate Heartfree and succeeds so well that Lady Fancyful becomes wildly jealous, resorts to desperate plots, and in the end compasses her own undoing. She also tries to injure Lady Brute by informing Sir John of his wife's interview with Constant near the arbor, but this move too turns to the advantage of Fancyful's enemies. It furnishes Belinda with a motive for accepting Heartfree, who has already laid his devotion at her feet. This love affair is the one example in Vanbrugh of the coquette's conquest of the beau, a predominant theme in the plays of Etherege and Congreve and the one by means of which the latter reached the high-water mark of English comedy; but Vanbrugh's scenes between these lovers are so blurred and hasty as to give the impression that he was practically uninterested in the situation. He has evidently gone one step farther in the realm of comedy than did his predecessors. They occupied themselves most of all with the eternal conflict between man and woman which normally

ends in betrothal and marriage; he began where they left
off and envisaged matrimony itself from the comic, not
like Wycherley from the satiric, point of view. In doing
so he provided himself with a larger canvas and, at the
same time, a more difficult one to cover satisfactorily.
Deeper feeling exists between husband and wife than between lovers, deeper feeling means greater dramatic possibilities, and yet deeper feeling tends to endanger the
comedian's art. This paradox plunged Vanbrugh into the
brutalities of Berinthia and Loveless as well as into the
sentimentalities of Amanda and Worthy, and it prevented him from indulging in airy and charming combats
of wit like those between Dorimant and Harriet Woodvil, Bellmour and Belinda (in *The Old Bachelor*), Mirabell and Millamant.

To make up for this loss, his clever dialogues take
place between two persons of the same sex, generally
ladies. The weakness of these interviews is that there is
no emotional drive behind the repartee; their strength lies
in the fact that no ulterior emotion interferes with the
dryness and sparkle of wit for wit's sake. It is true that
Berinthia is trying to debauch Amanda, but she does it
more because "it exercises almost all the entertaining fac-
ulties of a woman" than for any hopes she has of regain-
ing Worthy's affections. Besides, their most lengthy and
brilliant conversation takes place before Berinthia and
Worthy have laid their heads together to plan Amanda's
ruin. In it Berinthia is occupied with describing her way
of life: how she has twenty lovers, but not one secret one
among them; how one can easily manage a beau, but how
difficult it is to deal with a real man; how delicious a
thing it is to be a young widow; and how she has resolved
to marry again that she never may. Berinthia represents

the purely animal, pleasure-loving woman with keenness enough to see through the deceits of this world and sufficient intelligence to turn them to her own advantage. She would be an ideal comic character, if one could ever quite bring himself to believe in her existence. Vanbrugh himself never could, and by putting a figure like Amanda into the same play with her, he permits us to observe a substantial rift in the armor of his comedy. Amanda is too good to be true, but Berinthia is correspondingly too hard and too unemotional a being to be a credible personage.

Belinda in *The Provok'd Wife* is more human and less sparkling, but her conversational vis-à-vis makes up for her deficiencies in this respect. Lady Brute is so much cleverer than Amanda that she and Belinda together quite overreach the Amanda-Berinthia combination. In fact, for sheer dialogue, the scenes between Belinda and her aunt are the best things in all Vanbrugh. Belinda's rôle is to listen to the state of Lady Brute's feelings both towards her husband and Constant, and to make suitable observations on the relations of the sexes. "A woman's life would be but a dull business, if 'twere not for men," Lady Brute remarks, and Belinda replies, "Were there no men in the world, o' my conscience, I should be no longer a-dressing than I am a-saying my prayers. . . . No, if there were no men, adieu fine petticoats, we should be weary of wearing 'em."

Lady Brute. And adieu plays, we should be weary of seeing 'em.

Bel. Adieu Hyde-Park, the dust would choke us.

Lady Brute. Adieu St. James's, walking would tire us.

Bel. Adieu London, the smoke would stifle us.

Lady Brute. And adieu going to church, for religion would ne'er prevail with us.

Bel. Our confession is so very hearty, sure we merit absolution.

Then they go on discoursing about how a lady should act at the theatre when a nasty line is blurted out on the stage, a question of social etiquette already considered by Molière in *La Critique de l'École des Femmes* and by Wycherley in *The Plain Dealer.* Belinda says she daren't laugh, to look serious betrays one's understanding of the jest; so for her part she always takes the occasion to blow her nose! Such a debate is a long way from the plot of the play, but it is certainly amusing, and it reveals quite clearly Vanbrugh's attitude towards the female sex. In his early plays, at least, they are all cynical and disillusioned, if they are not sentimental and ingenuous.

It is to be remembered that when he wrote these first comedies Vanbrugh was still a bachelor, looking at women in general and matrimony in particular from the outside. By the time that he had embarked upon his last play, *A Journey to London*, he had taken unto himself a wife and, perhaps in consequence, he had become more charitable. Lady Arabella, to be sure, is still the absurd, selfish woman of the world, but her friend Clarinda expounds a theory of life that is eminently sensible and sane. In summer she would live in the country and ride soberly, walk soberly, sit soberly under a tree, garden soberly, read soberly, hear a little music soberly, converse soberly, work soberly, and manage her family soberly; in winter she would be in town: "I would entertain myself in observing the new fashions soberly, I would please myself in new clothes soberly, I would divert myself with agreeable friends at home and abroad soberly, I would play at quadrille soberly, I would go to court soberly, I would go to some plays soberly, I would go to operas soberly, and I think I could go once, or if I liked my company, twice to a masquerade soberly." There is, of course, a touch of satire in the repetition of the word "soberly," but the purpose of the whole speech is rather to serve as a background for Lady Arabella's comment on the masquerade: "If it had not been for that last piece of sobriety, I was going to call for some surfeit-water." This episode is typical of Vanbrugh's entire comic method: he sets before you the highest ideals of human conduct (sometimes they are so high as to be absurd), he shows you how far below them individuals ordinarily fall, and then—without malice and without displeasure—he laughs at the limitations of mankind.

V.

There is indeed no more marked contrast in human life than that between the loftiness and pettiness of feminine nature, and Vanbrugh never for a moment lets his audience forget this basic source of the comic. Amanda and Berinthia mark more obviously the same antithesis as Clarinda and Lady Arabella, nor is it always necessary to have the ideal present, in order to ridicule an imperfect realization of it. Lady Brute has within herself the elements of both fidelity and infidelity, but more frequently Vanbrugh's women are merely animals, like the *bourgeoises à la mode.* So it occurs that, often and often in his theatre, the physical side of female humanity is emphasized and its spiritual shortcomings are pointedly developed. In *Aesop*, Roger's wife has put him up to going to court, for "she has been so proud, so saucy, so rampant ever since I brought her home a laced pinner, and pink-colour pair of shoe-strings, from Tickledawne Fair, the parson o' th' parish can't rule her"; in *The Provok'd Wife*, Heartfree speaks his bachelor mind when he says that on examining a woman's heart, "I find there pride, vanity, covetousness, indiscretion, but above all things, malice"; and in *The Mistake*, Vanbrugh takes real delight in a spirited rendering of Molière's lines on the weaknesses of femininity. "I have been a servitor in a college at Salamanca, and read philosophy with the doctors," Sancho (Gros-René) tells his master, "where I found that a woman in all times, has been observed to be an animal hard to understand, and much inclined to mischief. Now as an animal is always an animal, and a captain is always a captain, so a woman is always a woman." A woman is always an animal to Sancho, and so she essentially is to a comic dramatist like Vanbrugh.

It is interesting to note how much more at home Sir John seems to be in the low-life passages from Molière than with the high-flown romantic sentiments in which the main plot of *Dépit Amoureux* abounds, and the same tendency may be observed in his other adaptations. It is curious that again and again he should choose a romantic play on which to exercise his talents: *Aesop*, *The Pilgrim*, *The False Friend*, and *The Mistake* are all taken from dramas (most of them in verse) filled with noble emotions and even nobler sentiments. Perhaps Vanbrugh kept on good terms with his conscience by devoting his energies to such elevated material and then pleased himself by the prosaic and ribald way in which he treated it. At any rate, each time that he had any real success with his second-hand work, it was in the coarser passages, where he could stick to mundane concerns and did not need to soar with his original into the higher levels of romantic fancy. Such passages are generally those in which the servants are concerned, and in every case Vanbrugh has added to and developed their rôles. Doris in *Aesop*, Jacinta, Lopez, and Galindo in *The False Friend*, Lopez and Sancho in *The Mistake*, but more especially Flippanta and Brass in *The Confederacy* have mere shadows as their prototypes.

In the last-named play the adapter was particularly skillful. Here he was dealing with material congenial to him, with bourgeois, not aristocratic, society, with creatures of flesh and blood, not of air and fantasy. As a result, he everywhere equals and often surpasses his model. Clarissa is more absurd in her ambitions than Dancourt's Angelique, Corinna more forward than Mariane, Mrs. Amlet (she has two whole new scenes) more vulgar and more doting than Mme. Amelin, Flippanta more active than Lisette, and Brass, "exquisite Brass," quite another person from Frontin. The French original is merely a servant; in Vanbrugh he is Dick Amlet's companion, who "passes for his Valet de Chambre." This rise in the social scale gives a chance for an extended amplification of the blackmailing scene and further points out the difference between what a man is and what he appears to be. Brass appears to be Dick's servant when he is really his equal; he appears to be a rogue, but the inner reality is something quite otherwise. At least, such an interpretation seems to fit in with Vanbrugh's conception of comedy as the absurd and petty modifications which the real, *i.e.*, the ideal, has to undergo in the course of an earthly existence.

From the very first he was absorbed by this notion. Are Loveless and Amanda to live a happy married life as

Cibber promised? Why, no, the Berinthias of this world will never permit it. Of course if virtue, not comedy, were to hold full sway, Loveless would also be saved from sin; but "real life is nothing at all like that." It may not be fitting to have Lady Brute cuckold her husband in the course of *The Provok'd Wife*, but after the play is over she is sure to do so. If Lady Headpiece is not won by her present admirer, she will be by a later one. Yet behind this cynicism and this laughter, Vanbrugh's kindly and fallible nature constantly asserts itself. Amanda's honor must be saved, Sir Tunbelly Clumsey will care about his daughter, the countryman in *Aesop* may be made to see the error of his ways, even Lady Headpiece is likely to relapse into virtue when once she gets back to her country home. The breath of fresh air and wholesome living constantly sweeps through Vanbrugh's plays, temporarily driving out of them the hardness and artificiality of town life. Nevertheless, Lord Foppington and Lady Fancyful still prevail upon the stage. It is they whom one remembers after the curtain has been rung down, and it is with them that the tradition of Wycherley and Congreve still continues in Vanbrugh's theatre.

Only upon second thought do we realize that in his plays there are no more sparkling love duos and that in them the harsh, uncompromising attack of Plain Dealers has come to an end. Women may be criticized out of their own mouths or out of other people's, but with this criticism there is always stated or implied the higher standards which they themselves could reach, if they only would. Like his characters, Vanbrugh is struggling. He is struggling to get out of the comic underworld and emerge into the pure light of perfection. Only, unfortunately, the perfection for which he strives is too often that of Amanda and Leonora (the impossibly righteous heroine of *The False Friend*), a vague and pallid reflection of stronger and worthier ideals. At bottom he would not achieve it if he could. He is more at home in the earthy society of Berinthia and Brass, Lord Foppington and Lady Fancyful, the Brutes and the Headpieces, than he is among the spotless heroes and heroines he has lifted from Fletcher, Le Sage, Molière, or Colley Cibber. He knows that to laugh at human foibles is not a satisfactory way to face the riddle of the universe, but his attempts to probe the deep emotions of mankind are faltering and pathetic. His inability to do so betrays his limitations but at the same time emphasizes his special abilities within a definitely circumscribed area. Failure to reach the spiritual heights is not discreditable to the comic dramatist; but one cannot help feeling regret when any author tries to free himself from the solid earth only to sink back into the mawkish mire of sentimentality. Sir John Vanbrugh's work, both in its strength and in its weaknesses, helps to define clearly and limit exactly the narrow sphere allotted in the world of art for the exclusive possession of the Comic Spirit.

GEORGE FARQUHAR
1678?—1707

O NE of the most striking facts about the dramatic work of George Farquhar is that, though his plays are generally classed with seventeenth-rather than eighteenth-century comedy, no one of them appeared before Jeremy Collier sounded the death-knell of the old order in 1698. It was in March of that year that the *Short View of the Profaneness and Immorality of the English Stage* struck terror into the hearts of such essentially comic dramatists as Congreve and Vanbrugh; almost immediately a new ally for them appeared on the London boards in the person of Farquhar, whose *Love and a Bottle* was acted late in 1698 or early in 1699. Also in 1699, the newcomer from Ireland brought forward *The Constant Couple; or, A Trip to the Jubilee*, a play in which Robert Wilks's performance of Sir Harry Wildair achieved a remarkable success. Two years later Farquhar produced a sequel to this popular piece, naming it after Wilks's now famous part; in 1702 he offered two new comedies to the public, *The Inconstant; or, The Way to Win Him*, adapted from Fletcher's *The Wild-Goose Chase*, and *The Twin-Rivals*. In the next four years his only contribution to the stage was *The Stage Coach* (1704), a one act farce, which with Peter Anthony Motteux he had adapted from Jean de la Chapelle's *Les Carosses d'Orléans*, but in 1706 he again made an important contribution to English dramatic literature. In fact, Farquhar's chief claim to fame rests upon his last two plays, *The Recruiting Officer*, produced in 1706, and *The Beaux-Stratagem*, acted in 1707. This last, his comic masterpiece, he composed while in a "settled sickness," which resulted in his death a few weeks after the première. His premature end has caused much idle speculation as to what he might have later accomplished, had his life been spared.

I.

What Farquhar did accomplish was to lift English Comedy from the Centre of Indifference in which it had been languishing under Vanbrugh's aegis and, for good or ill, to set it down in the freer aether of eighteenth-century sentiment. He is the connecting link between the older generation of the Restoration and the rising tide of Cibbers and Steeles, Kellys and Cumberlands, Goldsmiths and Sheridans. If to have one foot in each of two camps is a successful compromise, Farquhar is an outstanding success in his chosen field; if not to be wholeheartedly devoted to some one cause is cowardly and craven, Farquhar ignobly falls between two stools. He was an Irishman, and consistency is not to be expected of him, any more than it is to be found in his first important self-portraiture, Roebuck in *Love and a Bottle*. Roebuck is himself from Ireland, "of a wild roving temper," a gorgeous mixture of hard head and soft heart. We first see him, completely down and out, preparing to join the army, until a crippled ex-soldier tells him that there's nothing in it and that he better turn ruffian instead. We find almost immediately that Roebuck's predicament has been caused by his flight from Ireland, where his father wanted him to marry the mother of his two illegitimate children; also that he has quarreled with a virtuous lady with whom he was in love there, because he could not debauch her. He does his best to convert an upright friend to the "eat, drink, and be lewd" way of life, but this interview results in the friend's employment of Roebuck to test his own mistress, Lucinda. "She's a lady of eighteen, beautiful, witty, and nicely virtuous," Roebuck is told, to which he replies, "Witty and virtuous! ha! ha! ha! Why, 'tis as inconsistent in ladies as gentlemen."

It is certainly inconsistent in gentlemen if Roebuck himself be an example. Selfish and delightful as he appears in the first act, he is a very different person by the end of the play. At the beginning of it he is a comic figure, to be laughed at but not actively censured; later he is found to have a heart of gold and to be the very personification of honor. An attempt to reconcile these opposing tendencies of the comic and sentimental spirits is made in Leanthe's often quoted words about Roebuck: "Wild as winds, and unconfined as air!—Yet I may reclaim him. His follies are weakly founded, upon the principles of honour, where the very foundation helps to undermine the structure. How charming would virtue look in him, whose behaviour can add a grace to the unseemliness of vice!" Leanthe is the before-mentioned young Irish girl who has resisted Roebuck's unlawful importunities and then followed him to London disguised as a page. Of course, she ultimately succeeds in reclaiming him from vice and making him her own. Roebuck, though not anxious to be fettered, marries her under the impression that she is the rich Lucinda; and after the ceremony he is so enthralled that he is only too anxious to fight for her honor when it is called in question. That Lucinda changes into Leanthe does not seem to worry him at all, for in his heart of hearts he has always been true to the peerless lady who could resist his attractions. His cast-off mistress, whom with a touch of his earlier callousness he now addresses as "stale iniquity," is consoled with £500, which have been extorted from a rich country squire, and the curtain falls with the quondam rake's smugly satisfied statement:

> I have espoused all goodness with Leanthe,
> And am divorced from all my former follies.

Roebuck is Farquhar himself, or, at least, he is Farquhar's ideal type in its crudest form. Never again did the dramatist draw such an obviously inconsistent picture, although the contrast between honesty and knavery is present in most of his leading male figures. The most popular of them, perhaps because of Wilks's acting in the part, was the Sir Harry Wildair of Farquhar's second and third plays. Sir Harry, "the joy of the playhouse, and the life of the Park," has newly come from Paris at the opening of *The Constant Couple*. He is described before his entrance as a happy combination of bravery and gaiety, the latter a result of his free and easy education far removed from the pedantry of schools. He has in his make-up just a touch of the French beau's affectation, but, on the whole, he is an attractive figure, well-calculated to delight a pleasure-loving audience. Constancy is not one of his virtues, for at his first appearance he is in love with a dangerous lady whom he has encountered in Paris, but in the fifth act he is joined in matrimony to the insipid Angelica. His relations with this Angelica are based on a fundamental misunderstanding, which is the artificial mainspring of Farquhar's plot. A disappointed lover of Angelica's tells Sir Harry that her virtue is marketable, so that he attempts to purchase it for twenty, fifty, or a hundred guineas, "the prettiest goldfinches that ever chirped in a cage." In the final scene between them Sir Harry is drunk and importunate, Angelica shocked and outraged to such a point that her lover significantly remarks: "This is the first whore in heroics that I have met with." It is this falsity between the real and supposed character of Angelica which gives us Sir Harry as at once a comic and sympathetic character, even up to the moment where he marries her only to avoid a duel—as he says—and then raves about the charms of lovely woman.

In the sequel he is reduced to the rôle of a devoted husband. Angelica is supposed to be dead, and though Sir Harry is engaged in an intrigue with a former love, he will hear no word against his wife's reputation. He wishes to fight a French marquis who asserts that she was unfaithful, and he terminates his affair with the woman who has repeated this slander. In a word, Sir Harry's morality has triumphed over his gaiety, so that it is no wonder that the piece failed to repeat its predecessor's success. When Angelica reappears in male disguise, as a ghost, and finally in the flesh, a neat dénouement has been achieved and a worthy lesson inculcated, but honest laughter has long since flown out of the window. That Sir Harry has become a model and is no longer a humorous type, is made very clear by his renunciation of French foppery and also by a strange scene between him and a Lord Bellamy, which is injected into the play without any apparent connection with the rest of the plot. Lord Bellamy, it seems, owes Sir Harry two hundred guineas, lost by his wife at cards, but he is unwilling to pay them. He excuses himself on the grounds of being a "man of honour," a phrase that throws Sir Harry into a fury. "Honour! that's such an impertinence!" he screams,

"Pray, my lord, hear me. What does your honour think of murdering your friend's reputation? making a jest of his misfortunes? cheating him at cards, debauching his bed, or the like? . . . Come, come, my lord; no more on't, for shame; your honour is safe enough, for I have the key of its back-door in my pocket." The fact that Farquhar could put such a violent denunciation of conventional "honour" into the mouth of his hero and idol, Sir Harry Wildair, shows how very far he had got from the true Comic Spirit of moral detachment and unbiased laughter.

"Honour is a circumstance absolutely unnecessary in a natural correspondence between male and female," he wrote in his next play, *The Inconstant*, and similarly of "morals": "I tell thee, child, there is not the least occasion for morals in any business between you and I. Don't you know that of all commerce in the world there is no such cozenage and deceit as in the traffic between man and woman?" These words are put into the mouth of Young Mirabel, the inconstant hero, who is trying so hard to escape from his engagement with the lovelorn Oriana. "In a world where all is for the worst," he seems to say, "I myself will not alone be virtuous," which is one way of building a comic superstructure upon a basic discontent with the world. Many devices are used by Farquhar to reconcile his feeling for morality with his ability to entertain, since he was not able with the genius of a Molière to hold the two in suspended solution even for the two hours' traffic of the stage. The ability to draw human characters would make such a happy consummation as Molière's possible; the advantage of mannered types is that they may be tortured and twisted out of all consistency by the ingenuity of their creator. So without a thought of duplicity, Mirabel condemns society and then uses this condemnation to justify his own selfishness. For four acts he tells his father that he will not fulfill his promise to marry Oriana, and indeed he does everything in his power to escape her wiles. She, in turn, pursues him with all the ingenuity she can command: she produces a supposed lover to be his rival; she pretends to have become a nun; she feigns insanity; and finally she disguises herself as a page and follows the object of her devotion. The fifth act situation, in which she saves her lover from an adventuress and four bravoes, is an addition to Fletcher's comedy, founded, it is said, on an actual occurrence of the time. At any rate, it forms a most effective outcome for the play, even if it does change the general atmosphere from a leisurely picture of manners and customs to bustling intrigue and melodramatic action.

The true comedy spirit is better found in *The Inconstant* in the sub-plot of Duretete and Bisarre, each a combination of two characters taken from *The Wild-Goose Chase*. Duretete is too shy and Bisarre too coquettish, so their meetings are bound to be fraught with amusement to the spectators. These encounters begin with Bisarre's pleasing Duretete by an appearance of being learned and go on with her revenge on him when she has heard him say he is too much of a man of honor to marry her. She makes him dance and drink much against his will, pretends to be subservient only to laugh at him, and finally says she will follow him throughout the world whether he likes it or not. There is not much consistency in these scenes (somewhat because of the telescoping of Fletcher's material already referred to), but each is amusing in itself, one of the chief objectives and also one of the most frequent failings of comedy. Laughter in this world is sporadic and unorganized; it does not obey any of the rules that have come to be well-established canons of art. It cannot be expected then that the Comic Spirit shall always work with equal skill throughout the entire course of a play. Certainly the particular strand of plot under discussion has no distinct resolution. Bisarre says she won't marry Duretete, for "I like the beast well enough, but I don't understand his paces so well as to venture him in a strange road;" Duretete counters with, "There is but one thing should make me thy husband. I could marry thee today for the privilege of beating thee tomorrow;" to which hostile dialogue jolly Old Mirabel puts an end with his optimistic, "Come, come, you may agree for all this," an indeterminate solution which would never have done for the main plot of any well-regulated drama.

Farquhar's next play, *The Twin-Rivals*, is chiefly serious drama and very little, one regrets, true comedy. The author's moral sense is in the ascendant, as is shown at once by the "Preface." Virtue must be rewarded and vice punished, even if the characters are not of a heroic cast, a dictum which means the lowering of tragedy and the elevation of comedy to the no-man's land of heavy sentiment. *Comédie larmoyante* and bourgeois tragedy are closely connected, and *The Twin-Rivals* is a good example of the fact. Instead of a principal character obviously divided between high ideals and human weaknesses, like Roebuck, Wildair, or Mirabel, in this play we have divided persons also. The twin Wouldbes are the personifications of Good and Evil—even Benjamin's body is deformed as a symbol of his character—and, as a result, neither of them really interests us. It is clear from the first that the honest Hermes is to return and oust the dishonest Benjamin, that he will marry the heroine and conserve the paternal estate. One is not even surprised at the completeness of Benjamin's dismissal to poverty and contempt or at the consignment of his accomplices to prison and the pillory. Justice is seen done with a thoroughness that belongs to morality but not to life, and consequently not to the most perfect art.

Yet lest the lesson has not been sufficiently enforced, a minor plot also deals with the triumph of virtue over vice. Richmore is trying to marry his cast-off mistress to Trueman and at the same time to debauch Trueman's own beloved, Aurelia. Trueman himself is successful in rescuing Aurelia from a disreputable house and then confronts Richmore with the evidence of his guilt. "Truth, by Heavens! . . . Trueman, canst thou forgive me?" murmurs the repentant villain, and though while disarmed he scorns to yield, after Trueman has returned his sword he agrees to marry the girl he has forsaken. So once again the right prevails, this time in the breast of the converted wrong-doer. An ironic commentary on this phase of the happy ending occurs in Farquhar's "Preface," an attempt to defend his play from its many critics: "Some people are apt to say, that the character of Richmore points at a particular person; though I must confess I see nothing but what is very general in his character, except his marrying his own mistress; which, by the way, he never did, for he was no sooner off the stage but he changed his mind, and the poor lady is still *in statu quo*." This statement goes one step farther than Vanbrugh's remark that Constant in *The Provok'd Wife* has not got his mistress *yet*, for it not only suggests that the play continues after the fall of the curtain, but it positively reverses the action that has taken place upon the stage. It is a definite admission of insincerity on the author's part and serves to justify, if not altogether to explain, the indifference with which *The Twin-Rivals* was received by the public. The comparative failure of this piece may partially account for Farquhar's virtual withdrawal from play-writing during the next four years and also for the change of attitude that is noticeable in his last two comedies.

II.

The Recruiting Officer is not by any means a complete *volte-face* to the type of Congreve's comedy, but it definitely eschews the sermonizing of *The Twin-Rivals*. It is rather an attempt to return to Farquhar's own earlier successes with Roebuck and Wildair, to elaborate the figure of a well-meaning rake, and to set him in an environment giving more variety and scope for action. This milieu the dramatist found in the provincial town of Shrewsbury, where he had himself been in 1705 to get recruits for Marlborough's army. He justly dedicates his play "To all Friends round the Wrekin," for among them he had hit upon material which was to insure him a permanent place in the history of English comedy. Farquhar's early plays show a certain brilliant promise, but not till he forewent a criticism of town life and followed Vanbrugh's lead out into the freer air of the English countryside did he achieve his most solid and most genuine success. The hero of *The Recruiting Officer* (the Wilks part again) is Captain Plume, who like Roebuck and Richmore is introduced to us embarrassed with a cast-off mistress. "Molly at the Castle" has just borne a son to Plume but has been comforted in her misfortune by Plume's broad-minded sweetheart, the charming Silvia.

Silvia is the most delightful heroine in all Farquhar. Like so many of his ladies—Leanthe, Angelica, and Oriana—she has resisted her lover's desire for "consummation before the wedding," and like them she disguises herself as a boy, in order to subjugate the unwilling hero. While masquerading, she finds her lover flirting with Rose, a country girl, but neither angry nor discouraged she enters the lists as his rival. Under a threat of enlisting with another recruiting officer, she gets Rose away from Plume, enlists with him herself, and has firmly wormed her way into his heart by the time that the imposture is discovered. Also she has given her father an opportunity to find out that Plume had no designs against his daughter's honor, as a forged letter coupled with Plume's own disposition had quite naturally led him to believe. "I have got an air of freedom, which people mistake for lewdness in me," Plume himself says, and considering his past as represented by "Molly at the Castle" and his pre-nuptial proposition to Silvia, one can hardly be surprised at the misconception. Still, of all Farquhar's hero-rakes Plume is the most convincing, and we are ready to forgive his short-comings as outbursts of excess vitality and to believe that he really means it when in the last act he tells Silvia that to her love he resigns his freedom. Before Farquhar's time the question of a gentleman's honor had scarcely entered into English comedy, though Vanbrugh had rung the changes on woman's good name in Amanda, Berinthia, and most compactly of all in the character of Lady Brute. Etherege's heroes are rascals, it is true, and they ultimately bow their necks to the yoke of wedlock, but there is no indication that the idea of reformation ever entered their creator's head. For all we know the Comic Spirit will continue to play over Sir Frederick

Frollick and Dorimant long after they are married; in the case of Roebuck, Mirabel, and Plume such an outcome is absolutely incompatible with the melting mood in which we leave them. This new type of wild young man, ultimately to be domesticated by a lovely girl had been overshadowed by Vanbrugh in the subordinate figure of Worthy in *The Relapse*, but Farquhar gave him such vitality and distinction that he became a well-recognized and often repeated character in drama and in fiction. Charles Surface is no more than a weakened imitation of the same individual (as Lady Teazle is of the female of the species); Tom Jones only a well-rounded presentation of a similar figure in a more diffuse and complicated genre.

The Beaux-Stratagem, Farquhar's last comedy, furnished him with an opportunity to do the two sides of his usual picture in separate and distinct parts, just as Jacinto Benavente in a modern play, *The Bonds of Interest*, has created an idealistic master and a selfish servant to represent together the average human being. Aimwell and Archer, although contrasting figures, are not such extremely opposed types as the Wouldbe brothers in *The Twin-Rivals*, for they are both fortune-hunters and both travelling under false pretensions. Aimwell has the softer heart of the two, and just when he is on the point of successfully winning Dorinda, a rich heiress, his conscience asserts itself and he declares his true estate. Fortunately the high-minded Dorinda will allow his poverty to make no difference, and more fortunately still his elder brother, whom he was counterfeiting, has died in the nick of time, so he is now the true Viscount Aimwell. This stroke of luck brings the impecunious gentleman a fortune, large enough to support a wife in comfort, and enables him to give over Dorinda's own £10,000 to his practical-minded companion, Archer. Archer, who is no philanthropist, could not see any reason in the world for Aimwell's ultra-honesty, and when the affair is satisfactorily compounded, he has no intention at all of giving up his share in the booty. Archer is, in fact, a thorough rogue, and yet withal the most high-spirited and completely hilarious figure that Farquhar ever created.

We are first introduced to him passing as Aimwell's servant in the fortune-hunting adventure. No situation is too humiliating and too unpleasant for him, if only it leads to ultimate success and riches; "there is no scandal like rags, nor any crime so shameful as poverty," is the summary of his creed. Meanwhile, being a gay care-free dog, he makes the most of his temporary inferiority in the social scale. Alone with Aimwell, he asserts his individuality strongly (one is here reminded of Brass in *The Confederacy*); at other times he presumes upon his disguise to prosecute a love-affair with the buxom Cherry, daughter of the landlord of their inn. The amusing, if artificial, scene of "Love's Catechism" and Cherry's attempts to draw the supposed servant into marriage may be written in the "pert, low dialogue" for which Pope censured Farquhar, but they are also the forerunners of the more genteel interviews between Young Marlow and Kate Hardcastle.

Archer's more important love-affair is with Mrs. Sullen at the great house. She is the unhappy wife of a heavy country squire, bored to desperation away from town and only too anxious to take up with a new lover. She is already intriguing with a French count, when Archer appears upon the scene and by his dashing vivacity completely supersedes the foreigner. He manages to take the count's place in Mrs. Sullen's closet, reveals himself as she is about to retire, and in one of the most straightforward scenes in Restoration Comedy vanquishes her resistance. The Loveless-Berinthia model is not completely copied, however, for at the psychological moment Archer and Mrs. Sullen are interrupted by a cry of "Thieves!" They discover that the house is being robbed, and lovemaking has to yield to active defense. The next day Mrs. Sullen's brother appears and arranges her divorce, thus leaving her free to marry whom she will. Whoever that may be, one suspects that it will not be Archer, to whom love for a night is a very different proposition from love for a lifetime. He is a perfectly soulless character, eminently fitted to take the leading part in the last of English classic comedies. True, Farquhar has given him a conscientious friend and has prevented him from committing physical adultery; but, though Jeremy Collier might not think so, the spirit is more important than the flesh, and, to all intents and purposes, Archer and Mrs. Sullen have carried out their intrigue in the white light of reality. It is interesting to note Farquhar's saving clause, but more significant still to realize that hereafter in eighteenth-century comedy moral correctness was to come first and truth to intellectual processes must take a secondary position.

III.

It is also notable that Mrs. Sullen is not definitely provided with a mate at the end of the play, as are the ladies in all Farquhar's earlier comedies. Besides the rakish gentleman and his demure sweetheart, they generally contain another plot in which a woman difficult to please is the central figure. Through some misunderstanding or other

she is cruel to her true lover, he takes offense at her conduct, and some chance occurrence is necessary to resolve
the situation. This it may be seen is a typical romantic
plot, not dependent upon character or social conditions,
in which laughter plays a subordinate part and which is
taken quite seriously by Farquhar. Lucinda in *Love and
a Bottle* sees her suitor talking to Roebuck's mistress and
immediately jumps at conclusions; Aurelia in *The Twin-
Rivals* is insulted by Trueman's lack of respect for her;
Melinda in *The Recruiting Officer* grows haughty towards Worthy as a result of having inherited a fortune.
The various gentlemen endure the pangs of unrequited
love until Lucinda is convinced that it was all a mistake;
Aurelia is saved by Trueman from Richmore's attack;
and Melinda is converted to humility by the fortune-
telling hoax of Serjeant Kite. This last strand of plot is
as superior to its fellows as is the Plume-Silvia story to
its own early analogues. In *The Recruiting Officer* Farquhar had indeed struck his best comic stride: Melinda's
disdain has in it a gleam of personality, and Kite as a
conjuror furnishes a most entertaining bit of hokum. Mr.
Worthy, it is true, is a mere lay figure, but his rival, Captain Brazen, is, as we shall see, sharply individualized.

Farquhar's most elaborate form of this cruel lady story
is that from which *The Constant Couple* takes its name.
Lady Lurewell is the scornful lady *par excellence*, and
the cause of her hard-heartedness is diabolically ingenious. As she confides to her maid, she has been ruined at
the age of fifteen by a handsome young man who promised marriage and never reappeared. Like Madam Fickle
in D'Urfey's play of that name, she has resolved to break
all hearts and herself to remain scot-free from emotion.
Vengeance is her motive, and throughout the play she

steers a triumphant course, until she recognizes the ring which she had once given to her betrayer. Wildair possesses it at the time of her discovery, but she later finds that it really belongs to another of her innumerable pursuers. He is confronted with the charge of desertion and at once admits it, exclaiming, "The blest remembrance fires my soul with transport—I know the rest—you are the charming she, and I the happy man." He then tells a long story, explaining how he was prevented from returning, how he has sought her everywhere, and how his intentions have always been strictly honorable. Lurewell falls into his arms, but in the sequel Farquhar has had to make her a flighty wife to keep up the character which his audience had come to expect from a lady of her name. Angelica's ghost frightens her back into repentance, and again we are left with the cockles of our hearts supposedly warmed by reformation and good intentions. Yet there is very little matter for mirth to be found here, unless it lies in the inherent absurdity of the whole situation.

Quite otherwise is the case with Lurewell's numerous unsuccessful suitors in the earlier play. Here are the amusing Alderman Smuggler and his villainous nephew, Vizard; Smuggler, crying "Buss and guinea, buss and guinea," is a particularly excellent comic type. Lady Lurewell promises to receive him if he will come to see her dressed as an old nurse, she then palms him off on Vizard as herself, and thus the nephew's hypocrisy and deceit are revealed to his uncle. Later Smuggler himself is caught up with and put in jail because of some silver spoons which are found upon his person. Finally he receives a lecture on the sin of avarice and the difficulty of being a reformer. "Would you be thought a reformer of the times," Angelica tells him, "be less severe in your own censures, less rigid in your precepts, and more strict in your example." In jail Smuggler meets his old apprentice, Clincher Senior, now set up for a beau, in fact the "Jubilee beau" from whom the play takes its sub-title, *A Trip to the Jubilee.* Clincher has also been a suitor of Lurewell's, and association with her has landed him in prison too. She has made him change suits with a porter to avoid being discovered in her house; the porter's wife thinks he must have murdered her husband and prefers charges against him. Meanwhile his countrified brother, Clincher Junior, is told that the "Senior" has been killed, and he immediately assumes a fine gentleman's clothes and airs. These episodes provide opportunity for some little horseplay and considerable incidental satire, until the real beau is at last released from prison and once more affirms his resolution to set out for the Jubilee. In the sequel he has turned politician and runs stark mad after news and politics, but in this, as in every other particular, *Sir Harry Wildair* is much inferior to its predecessor.

The prototype of Clincher is to be found in the Mockmode of Farquhar's first play, *Love and a Bottle.* This pseudo-beau has not been an apprentice, but he has just come up from the University, a fact which only aggravates his absurd pretensions. He is most anxious to learn the ways of the polite world and, in order to do so, takes lessons from a pair of fencing and dancing masters, who quarrel about their relative professions quite in the vein of *Le Bourgeois Gentilhomme.* His landlady persuades him to buy champagne and to get drunk; he is made to think that a common whore is his divine Lucinda; he gives £100 to marry her and then £500 more to have it proved that the parson was no-parson. This last deceit is engineered by Lyric, an impecunious poet, who lives in the same lodging house as Mockmode, and who is one of Farquhar's most successful minor figures. He composes a burlesque on Nathaniel Lee's rant, is dunned by a land-lady whom he no longer wishes to placate with the shows of affection, gets a recalcitrant bookseller arrested for debt in his place, and frequently converses about his art—and incidentally that of Farquhar. "The hero in comedy is always the poet's character," says he, "a com-pound of practical rake and speculative gentleman, who always bears off the great fortune in the play, and shams the beau and squire with a whore or chambermaid: and as the catastrophe of all tragedies is death, so the end of comedies is marriage." This is a succinct and inclusive summary of Farquhar's comic formula, which was first employed for Roebuck in this same play, developed (without the beau and squire) in Mirabel, "The Incon-stant," and brought to a triumphant culmination with Plume in *The Recruiting Officer*. Archer's divergence from type in carrying off the heroine's fortune but not her person is, as we have seen, only a minor and welcome variation on the usual theme.

IV.

Just as these last plays reflect the best of Farquhar's work in their central situations, so do they, on the whole, contain his most varied and original subordinate charac-ters. Lyric is not too bad a creation, nor the pert servant "Jubilee Dicky" in *The Constant Couple*, nor peppery Old Mirabel in *The Inconstant*, nor the Irishman Teague nor the midwife Mrs. Mandrake in *The Twin-Rivals*, good acting parts all of them. It is, however, in the country setting of *The Recruiting Officer* and *The Beaux-Stratagem* that the dramatist found the most fertile material for his art. In the earlier of these two plays we have the bluff country justice, the innocent country girl, her blockhead of a brother, a butcher, a smith, and two priceless recruits, Coster Pearmain and Thomas Appletree by name. The first scene, in which Serjeant Kite is making a speech to his prospective victims, sets the tone of the comedy, and indeed all the recruiting scenes are marvels of invention and verve. Giving money under false pretenses, prosecuting love-affairs, telling fake fortunes, impressing dishonest officials, every conceivable method of obtaining soldiers is grist to Kite's mill, "so that if your worship pleases to cast up the whole sum, viz., canting, lying, impudence, pimping, bullying, swearing, whoring, drinking, and a halberd, you will find the sum total amount to a recruiting serjeant." Such is Kite's own exposure of his profession, as amusing but as undramatic in the context as that of Chaucer's Pardoner. Kite's master, Plume, is less an officer than a *jeune premier* lover; the other recruiting captain, Brazen, less an officer than a fool. He is the false beau, Congreve's Tattle or Witwoud, in a uniform, boastful of his military and amorous exploits, cocksure of himself, and gullible to the last degree. His deception by Lucy at once recalls the similar trick played by a similarly named maid-servant on one Sir Lucius O'Trigger, a further evidence of Farquhar's influence upon his imitative successors.

He himself had freshness and originality of invention. *The Recruiting Officer* has its varied rural and army characters; but *The Beaux-Stratagem* contains even more contrasting and unusual personages. Archer and Aimwell represent London; Lady Bountiful and her household, the Lichfield gentry; Bellair and Foigard, the army; Gibbet and his friends, the lawless gentlemen of the road; Boniface and Cherry, the small tradespeople, in this particular case the keepers of an inn. Lady Bountiful is, as her name implies, a benevolent old lady, particularly interested in curing diseases and quite blind to the limitations of her son, Squire Sullen. Sullen is the heavy type of drunken sot, who married only to get an heir to his estate and, being disappointed, treats his wife abominably. Mrs. Sullen is the vaporish fine lady, removed out of her proper environment and pining to get back to it. Her lover, Count Bellair, is a French prisoner at Lichfield, characterized chiefly by gallantry and an accent. The priest, Foigard, sets up to be a Frenchman too but is really an Irishman in disguise (Teague in *The Twin-Rivals* and Macahone in *The Stage Coach* are other examples of the delight that Farquhar took in drawing his own countrymen). Foigard's rival, Scrub, is an irrepressible man of all work, Gibbet a fine type of independent highwayman. Boniface with his "as the saying is" and the demure but sophisticated Cherry complete as attractive a gallery of stage portraits as are to be found in any English comedy. No wonder that these parts, coupled with that of the incomparable Archer, made *The Beaux-Stratagem* a great favorite with audience and actors alike. Its success was established on its first performance, and it held the stage in England and America for well over a hundred years.

It is idle to speculate on what Farquhar might have added to English drama had his life been spared, though it seems likely that he might have again equalled, if not surpassed, his now extant work. Certainly in his last illness his creative faculty was operating at fever heat. Even as it is, the author of *The Recruiting Officer* and *The Beaux-Stratagem* need have no fear for his place in literature; the originality and fertility of his imagination had destined him to be a superlative creator of comic figures. From Mockmode and Lyric in his earliest play to Sullen and Scrub in his latest, his pages are peopled with clearly defined persons, sure of provoking laughter whenever and wherever they are bodied forth upon the stage. Unhappily most of his works also contain a pseudo-romantic plot of cruel ladies and unhappy lovers, which seriously interferes with the end and aim of comedy. Lucinda, Aurelia, and Melinda are the airy names which betray the comic dramatist as being also a man of sentiment. "Lady Lurewell" is a more explicit epithet because her character is more realistically developed and hence more palpably absurd.

The real conflict in Farquhar's soul is most clearly visible in his treatment of his wild, young heroes. Roebuck, Wildair, Mirabel, and Plume, with their deserted whores and faithful mistresses, represent his constant attempt to paint the laughable and, at the same time, the admirable. Now this cannot be done, for as Aristotle well said in the *Poetics*, laughter implies some defect or ugliness contrary to the ideal. The two elements of license and honor are so contrasted in Roebuck's nature that he does not seem to be a credible human being. Wildair is better in reconciling the paradox, and Plume most successful of all. Yet there is always at bottom the feeling that these care-free, dashing young men are true neither to real life nor to the world of art. They are not human beings like Mercutio nor intellectual creations like Alceste; they are struggling between two worlds and will not commit themselves to either one. Occasionally an Archer steps completely into the comic picture, but then by his side there is always an Aimwell to spout high morality or a Gibbet to interfere with the impulses of nature. Archer is the last effort of the Comedy of Manners to maintain its position in the teeth of Jeremy Collier and eighteenth-century propriety. It was a losing fight though, as Farquhar must himself have realized. Try to follow his humorous impulses as he would, he always ended by throwing a sop to his morality-loving audiences. His works look forward to the complete triumph of sentimentalism upon the stage. They mark, at one and the same time, the last stand and —temporarily at least—the dying hope of the English Comic Spirit.

RELATIVE POSITION OF
RESTORATION COMEDY

I.

THE playwrights of the Restoration, as I have tried to show, represent the most refined development of the Comic Spirit in English drama, though comedy has always been present in our theatre. Even in the early religious miracle plays one finds the evidence of a crude, elementary sense of humor. Mak's passing off a stolen sheep as a child and his subsequent tossing in a sheet, from the Towneley *Second Shepherds' Play*, are primitive manifestations of the spirit of farce serving to enliven an otherwise intrinsically serious situation with one boisterous touch of nature. That such rough-and-tumble fun must have been amusing to the audience and hence satisfactory to the playwright is to be deduced from the fact that rarely since that time has a strain of physical incongruity been absent from English comedy. The Vice in the morality plays, Bobadill, Launcelot Gobbo, Tony Lumpkin, Bob Acres, and even *The Importance of Being Earnest* or *Arms and the Man* bear continued testimony to the prevalence of the farcical idea in our theatre. Any season in London or New York will afford abundant examples of this kind of dramatic writing, with which because of its very obviousness it is far easier to please for an age than for all time. The Comedy of Situation merely is elementary, and it is perennial, but the forms under which it appears must inevitably be legion.

To insure relative permanency for any comic material, it is necessary to differentiate characters and thus to make the various situations dependent upon the kind of persons who take part in them. The distinct figures of Herod and Pilate in the mysteries, for instance, are a faltering attempt to do the sort of thing, classically achieved by Ben Jonson in his comedy of "humours." His method was to seize upon and amplify the salient characteristic of a miser, a cheat, a blusterer, or a Puritan, whence it follows that Volpone is never anything but miserly, Captain Face spends his entire time in cheating simpletons, Bobadill is always ready to lord it over the craven, and Zeal-of-the-land Busy continually wants to reform the world. The weakness in this method of writing comedies is that your audience soon becomes aware that the persons on the stage are not what they pretend to be. Granted that they are not mere sticks with names attached to them, they are only sticks draped with a single quality, not live people, complex and inconsistent, such as we know in the world about us. Hence Shakespeare showed his genius in following Nature herself and not the rules of Art, though in so doing he removed his work from any definite aesthetic category, like that presided over by the Comic Spirit. Across the channel the clear-minded Molière appreciated Ben Jonson's difficulty and consciously tried to overcome it. The direct statement of his theory on this point occurs in *La Critique de l'École des Femmes*, à propos of Arnolphe's generosity to Horace as contrasted with his jealousy of Agnès, where it is written: "Il n'est pas incompatible qu'une personne soit ridicule en de certaines choses et honnête homme en d'autres." A comparison of Harpagon with Volpone will show how much farther from type and how much nearer to humanity Molière reached than his closest parallel in English literature. The philosophic Comedy of Character was not destined to attain to its full perfection upon British soil.

It is now a well-received opinion that Molière is much closer in spirit to his English predecessors, Ben Jonson and the school of Ben, than he is to the Restoration Dramatists. They were affected by both these influences, but with them the idea of comedy had changed in accordance with changed political and social conditions. After the closing of the theatres in 1642 and the period of Puritan repression, a violent reaction in art as well as morals was ushered into theatrical circles by the Restoration of Charles II to the English throne. The Stuart court during its sojourn on the Continent had observed the art of enjoying life, and on returning to England, its members intended to make up for the lean years of their exile by putting into practice what they had seen abroad—but by doing so without taste and, without moderation. They were in no mood to allow their plays to be dominated by heavy-handed moralizing in the vein of Father Ben; they stated that their work was to be, like his, "a discouragement of vice and folly," but what most of them really strove for was the sparkle and vivacity which they had watched upon the French stage.

Then ensued an age of drama without moral restrictions, and, worse than that, without a regard for fundamental ethical problems. As a logical result, it could not but be a superficial literature. Interest in the comic in human nature gave place to emphasis on the comic in society; Sir Fopling Flutter, Witwoud, and Lord Foppington derive their spirit from *Les Précieuses Ridicules* rather than from *Tartuffe*. The English dramatists tried now and again to touch on more serious matters, but when they did so, they generally strayed into the field of satire or sentiment. They seemed unable to keep for long at a time in the *juste milieu* of comic detachment. Yet their very defect was an integral part of their quality. A rarefication of material till it has achieved a tenuity, at any moment ready to snap, is the essence of the work of Etherege and Wycherley, of Congreve, Vanbrugh, and Farquhar. It is the most refined manifestation of the Comic Spirit, exquisite for the moment of its existence, but transitory, unstable, and episodic. The wheel soon comes full circle with the rise of sentimentalism, comedy is broken down into its natural components (the raw material of life), and the process of building it up must begin anew. The Comedy of Manners is, prior to the modern Comedy of Ideas, the last and most brilliant effort of the laughing muse to resist the intrusions of the more serious concerns of existence.

II.

Sir George Etherege unconsciously inaugurated this last phase. The titles of his three plays illustrate the variety of his attack: *The Comical Revenge* (*Love in a Tub*) centres in a purely farcical situation, the physical humors of Dufoy encased in a tub to avenge the displeasure of a waiting-maid; *She Would if She Could* has a more involved intrigue, which brings in the commonest of all Restoration plots, a deceivable husband and a wife ready to deceive; *The Man of Mode*, better known by its sub-title of *Sir Fopling Flutter*, takes up the beau of the period and ridicules him, as Etherege had already successfully done with the woman of fashion (my Lady Cockwood) in his second play. Yet in each of these comedies the chief interest is not really in the titular plot but in a

minor situation common to all of them. This is itself a
peculiarly significant fact. When one discovers a fine gentleman embarrassed with debts and mistresses meeting a
fine lady, who is already in love with him, succumbing to
her fascination, reluctantly declaring his feelings, and receiving an assurance of her affection only under protest—
and these events repeated in each of three comedies—one
realizes that here lies the key to Etherege's distinction.
He had discovered that one of the most fruitful sources
of mirth in a superficial, sophisticated civilization is the
occasional emergence in it of a very genuine emotion; and
by three times depicting that incongruous relationship
he made it his contribution to the history of English
comedy.

William Wycherley went deeper and accomplished
more. Starting with mistaken identities and disguised
lovers in his early plays, he soon found that his bent was
in the direction of satire. In *Love in a Wood*, he showed
us Addleplot made ridiculous by Dapperwit, Dapperwit
in turn fooled by Martha, Alderman Gripe and Lady
Flippant duped by that precious pair of bawds, Mrs. Joyner and Mrs. Crossbite. In *The Gentleman Dancing-Master*, the attack on national foibles and their imitators is
carried on by means of Don Diego and Monsieur de
Paris, but the fate meted out to neither one is the direct
result of his failing. In *The Country Wife*, however,
Wycherley evolved a fable which exactly illustrated his
central idea. Pinchwife, the jealous husband, is cuckolded
by the indomitable Horner and goes through the various
comic states of security, fear, and doubt. The idea that
one must not be jealous in matrimony is pushed home
more violently but less convincingly in the Sparkish sub-
plot. Horner's success with the Fidget and Squeamish

ladies is the final evidence as to how human nature will overcome convention in matters of sex. Not one mortal weakness, but all of them are the subject of attack in *The Plain Dealer*. The society which Wycherley here depicts (Olivia, Novel, Plausible, and the others) is too unredeemed by goodness to be credible, just as Manly, the protagonist, is too perfect not to be disagreeable. His isolation from his fellow beings is also essentially ridiculous, as we realize when we compare him with Molière's Alceste. M. Perromat in his recent study of Wycherley has tried to insist that this comparison is odious, because Wycherley was attempting something different from Molière; but he admits that this difference comes from the limitation of the Englishman's range. Alceste as well as his environment is under fire; Manly is represented as merely an antithesis to his vicious surroundings. Molière was content to show his misanthrope as honest and absurd at the same time; Wycherley would have one think that to be honest is to be admirable under all circumstances. Only here he fails, for Manly, instead of being the *beau ideal* that his creator intended, is a boor and a brute in his uncompromising attack upon the human race. In *The Plain Dealer*, comedy has passed into satire, and satire has overleapt itself, until its ferocity has made detestable the very things which it most wished to commend.

William Congreve started out to imitate the satire of Wycherley, though one soon finds him much more nearly in sympathy with the trifling spirit of Etherege. *The Old Bachelor* contains a Manly (Heartwell) and a Horner (Bellmour), but Bellmour, in his relations with Belinda, also represents Etherege's favorite hero, whose fate it always is to be subjugated by a clever woman. The Fondlewife plot follows *The Country Wife* quite closely, but not in the thoroughly satirical spirit of that masterpiece; beguiled husbands are stock figures in Congreve's theatre (Fondlewife, Lord Plyant, Lord Froth, and Foresight are all examples), but there is only the faintest criticism implied by the dry comic manner in which they are portrayed. The chief error in *The Old Bachelor* is, on the whole, the multiplicity of its plots, a defect which Congreve tried to remedy in his second play, *The Double-Dealer*. In his initial venture the construction had been too diffuse, here it was too compressed, and as a result the play failed most dismally. In his next effort, *Love for Love*, he hit upon the best story to be found in any of his comedies, even though the psychology of Angelica is slightly confused; but in his last work, *The Way of the World*, he reverted to the complexities of *The Double-Dealer*.

The truth is that Congreve was less interested and less skillful in structure than in elaborating the comic love duos of Etherege: Vainlove and Araminta in *The Old Bachelor* are only sketches, but Belinda's treatment of Bellmour in the same play is masterly and presaged greater triumphs; the wit of Mellefont and Cynthia in *The Double-Dealer* is rather cramped by the necessity of the plot that they shall not quarrel; Valentine and Angelica in *Love for Love*, on the other hand, are not yet declared lovers; but with Mirabell and Millamant in *The Way of the World* comes the true vindication of Congreve's genius—they admit that they care for one another, and yet they are constantly at war. As Shakespeare had found in *Much Ado About Nothing*, this paradoxical situation offers the dramatist a splendid opportunity to exercise his greatest talent, the expression of human feeling under the cover of conversational wit. Unfortunately there are few moments in life or in a five act play when such a chance occurs, and for the most part Congreve's cleverness goes off in set fireworks without any underlying dramatic necessity.

The Sharper-Belinda gossip off-stage in *The Old Bachelor* gives a key to the scenes of artificial wit in its author's last three comedies: Brisk, Tattle, and Witwoud could hardly exist at all except as a vehicle for brilliant dialogue. Congreve himself evidently spied a danger and tried to throw upon the audience the responsibility for any possible misapprehension as to these characters, when he wrote in the "Dedication" to *The Way of the World*, "This play had been acted two or three days, before some of these hasty judges could find leisure to distinguish between the character of a Witwoud and a Truewit." Perhaps the basic trouble was that Congreve himself could not clearly distinguish between the true and the false wit, because wit was to him an essentially forced and unnatural thing. At any rate, the Witwouds dominate his comedies, and one feels that if he had only been able to create more and better Truewits, he would rank far higher as a literary artist. As it is, one recognizes in him genius of the first order for writing dialogue that snaps and crackles, sometimes (it must be confessed) like thorns beneath a pot. His touch is of the lightness that tends towards superficiality and of the deftness necessary for those who play with gossamers.

Sir John Vanbrugh could draw the bow of Congreve no more tightly, so he gradually loosened the tight hold of comedy upon life. The important thing about him is not that he treated sentimentality from the comic point of view, but that he treated it at all. In his romantic adaptations, as well as in his sequel to *Love's Last Shift*, Vanbrugh is trying to spread the mantle of comedy over intrinsically non-comic material. The significant development in his first play, *The Relapse*, is not the weakness of Loveless, but the strength of Amanda; from now on marital infidelity must not be treated lightly by the Comic Muse. This is notable in *The Provok'd Wife*, where Lady Brute's intrigue with Constant is never definitely resolved; it is obvious in *The Confederacy*, with the wives' final renunciation of mischief-making; it gives one pause for consideration as to what would have been the dénouement of the unfinished *A Journey to London*. In the future the evils of the town are not to be shown upon the stage without an equivalent picture of the virtues of the country. To compensate for a Lord Foppington, drawn in the finest spirit of satire, there must be a Sir Tunbelly Clumsey, sympathetically and humanly presented; for an Aesop, masquerading as a beau, a Polidorus Hogstye; for a Lady Fancyful, a Miss Hoyden, although it must be admitted that in the last case Vanbrugh came very near to approximating the comic ideal. There are reminiscences of Congreve's wit dialogues in Vanbrugh's plays too, but only in the case of Heartfree and Belinda in *The Provok'd Wife* have they any emotional background. Amanda and Berinthia, Lady Brute and Belinda, Clarinda and Lady Arabella, discuss together the world and his wife, but as there is no conflict of sex, there must be a consequent loss of dramatic material in these scenes. In them is always present or implied, however, the difference between women at their best and at their worst, which at least lends variety to the conversation and which interests us as to the author's own state of mind. He continually oscillated between picturing the virtue in human nature that should be copied and the vice which should be ridiculed; he is just the reverse of Wycherley in deviating from the comic point of view, not by being too narrow, but by being too broad, not by expressing too much condemnation for evil, but by showing too much partiality for good.

George Farquhar diverged even farther than Vanbrugh from the golden mean of comedy. His leading figures, men rather than women, are strange combinations of comic defects and noble qualities. Incidentally they are almost all modelled on the temperamental young Irishman who created them. Roebuck in *Love and a Bottle* is the first rough sketch of a high-minded rake; Sir Harry Wildair in *The Constant Couple* is more entertaining and (in the sequel) more moral than Roebuck; Mirabel in *The Inconstant* finds the world an unmoral place and so justifies his own reluctant unscrupulousness; the Wouldbes in *The Twin-Rivals* each represent one half of the paradox, the villainous Benjamin being mirrored by a secondary character, Richmore, until the latter's repentance ranges him on the side of the virtuous Hermes. All these early plays of Farquhar's are really only experimental preparations for his last two comedies, *The Recruiting Officer* and *The Beaux-Stratagem*, in which the same idea is developed in a more finished way. Plume is the best of the hero-rakes, as Silvia is much the most attractive and natural of the heroines that reform them. Archer does not pretend to a vast amount of virtue, but he is high-spirited and likable; moreover, his conscientious companion, Aimwell, and the interruption to his illicit love-making preserve—artificially it is true—his integrity in the social scheme. From Farquhar's elaborate, and sometimes awkward, contrivances to reconcile the admirable and the reprehensible, it can be seen how hard he has had to struggle to maintain a comic attitude in the face of the encroachments of sentimentality.

His minor plots make the case even more plain, for the difficult lady who generally figures in them is frankly a romantic character. Lucinda, Aurelia, Melinda, and, most strikingly, Lady Lurewell have fallen out with their lovers through some misunderstanding, so that circumstances, not character, are responsible for the suffering which they cause and often share. Around these ladies are grouped a mass of minor figures who are genuinely comic and who illustrate very clearly Farquhar's gift for creative portraiture. Smuggler, Vizard, and the Clinchers in *The Constant Couple* are all suitors of Lady Lurewell's, Mockmode in *Love and a Bottle* has pretensions to Lucinda's hand, and Captain Brazen in *The Recruiting Officer* sighs for Melinda. Besides these unsuccessful suitors there are many other distinct personages strewn through the pages of Farquhar, servants, fathers, country folk, justices, highwaymen, and inn-keepers. They all have the vitality and life which keep their creator's comedies from being of the sentimental school, but they are at best but episodic figures. Farquhar marks the passing of the old order, just as Etherege had signalized its beginning.

III.

It is a brief development that commences in 1664 with *The Comical Revenge* and ends forty-three years later with *The Beaux-Stratagem*. (The posthumous *A Journey to London* need not be allowed to disturb the chronology.) It began with the reign of Charles II, extended through those of his successors James and William, and came to a definite conclusion in the times of Queen Anne.

Its genesis was the social life of the day, influenced by the literary tradition of Ben Jonson in England and of Molière in France. The comedy of "humours," or of character, is here taken over merely from the external side. Etherege was not interested in what his lovers were really like, but only in what they did and how that might be made entertaining to his audiences. Wycherley had the more serious purpose of criticizing the society in which he moved, but in overdoing his invective he annihilated its effect, save only in *The Country Wife*. Vanbrugh, on the other hand, strayed into the easy ways of sentimentality, and Farquhar followed him along that primrose path. There remains Congreve, who, with all his failings in plot structure and artificial wit, exhibits better than any other writer of English drama the essence of the Comic Spirit. His range is narrow, but in a restricted area his execution is superb. Could he have sustained the pitch of the love scenes in *The Way of the World* throughout an entire comedy, one would have acclaimed him the equal of Molière.

As it is, however, we must admit his inferiority, for the quality of those scenes is such that it cannot be long maintained. Even in them the wit sparkles sometimes with an unnatural lustre, and the difference between a conscious straining for effect and the serene sureness of a great artist cannot be better appreciated than by comparing the Mirabell-Millamant scenes with those between Alceste and Célimène in *Le Misanthrope*. Congreve's characters talk for talk's sake, Molière's because they are what they are; the charm of Célimène is always from within, that of Millamant chiefly from without. Célimène is a person, who to the end of the play keeps her individuality and freedom; Millamant capitulates easily, despite all the barbed darts of her conversation. As George Meredith says in his famous essay: "What she utters adds to her personal witchery, and is not further memorable . . . Célimène's is a woman's mind in movement, armed with an ungovernable wit."

Such seems to be the inherent difference between the master, Molière, and his English pupils, the Restoration Dramatists. The same contrast is noticeable in considering *The Country Wife*, Wycherley's best comic production, with its French prototype, *L'École des Femmes:* Horner has not the delicacy of Horace, Margery entirely lacks Agnès's development as love grows in her heart, and Pinchwife creates none of the sympathy that, in spite of one's self, one must feel for Arnolphe. In short, the French characters are human beings with human limitations, but also with human potentialities; Wycherley's creations are, in comparison, puppets set up to impersonate respectively Jealousy, Innocence, and the Life Force. Yet *The Country Wife* is Wycherley's most successful production, as *The Way of the World* is Congreve's, and these two plays represent the finest flowering of Restoration Comedy. They are to be depreciated only in comparison with Molière—to contrast purely comic writers with the universal genius of a Shakespeare is manifestly unfair—but by the same token they throw important light on the greatness of the Frenchman. Although it has not been definitely proved, it is a generally accepted supposition that Etherege must have travelled in France in his youth; we know that Wycherley was educated there and that Vanbrugh was imprisoned in the Bastille as an English spy. If these men were not entirely successful in transporting the *esprit gaulois* across the Channel, their attempt to do so is none the less evident.

When one notices, too, that neither Congreve nor Farquhar is a pure product of the island of Britain, one wonders if there can be any significance in the fact. Congreve went to school in Ireland with Swift, and Farquhar was born at Londonderry; not one of the Comic Dramatists of the Restoration can be said to be untouched by Gallic or Celtic influences. Is it just possible that the adroit touch of the Comic Spirit does not find itself at home in the theatre of tough-fibred Anglo-Saxons? One reflects that Germany has not produced any comedies that can rank for a minute with those of Molière, and that beside them the best efforts of Englishmen quickly sink into second place. The rough elements of farce seem to be congenial to John Bull's temperament, but his attempts to introduce character into funny situations never rise much higher than the "humours" of Ben Jonson. Although the roots of Restoration Comedy are to be found in native drama, foreign influences, both social and artistic, are in some degree responsible for it; from Etherege to Farquhar, the authors whose work we have been considering tried to refine upon the common sense of Molière and ended by creating a brightly colored bubble of thin substance and temporary duration. Yet, whatever its implications may be, it is certainly an indisputable fact that among English writers for the theatre William Congreve and, to a lesser degree, William Wycherley have best captured—if only for a moment—the elusiveness and grace, the gaiety and the detachment that are inextricably to be associated with the Comic Spirit.

INDEX